The Seal of the Prophets and His Message:

Lessons on Islamic Doctrine

(BOOK TWO)

Sayyid Mujtaba Musavi Lari

Translated by:
Hamid Algar

ISBN: 871031-35-4

Musavi Lari, Mujtaba.
    [Khatam-i anbiya va payamash. English]
    The Seal of the Prophets and his message : lessons on Islamic
doctrine/Mujtaba Musavi Lari: translated by Hamid Algar.
      p. cm. -- (The foundations of Islamic doctrine: v. 1)
      Translation of: Khatam-i anbiya va payamash.
      Series statement from CIP p. 7.
      Includes bibliographical references (p.   )
      ISBN 1-871031-35-4
      1. Muhammad, Prophet, d. 632. 2. Shi'ah--Doctrines. I. Algar, Hamid.
II. Title. III. Series: Musavi Lari, Mujtaba. Mabani-i i'tiqadat dar Islam.
English: v. 1.
      BP194.M8413 vol. 1
      [BP166.5]
      297'.2042 s--dc20
      [297'.63]   89-26785
                          CIP

Islamic Education Center
7917 Montrose Road
Potomac, MD 20854

Contents

About the Author

Sayyid Mujtaba Musavi Lari is the son of the late Ayatullah Sayyid Ali Asghar Lari, one of the great religious scholars and social personalities of Iran. His grandfather was the late Ayatullah Hajj Sayyid Abd ul-Husayn Lari, who fought for freedom in the Constitutional Revolution. In the course of his lengthy struggles against the tyrannical government of the time, he attempted to establish an Islamic government and succeeded in doing so for a short time in Larestan.

Sayyid Mujtaba Musavi Lari was born in 1314/1925 in the city of Lar where he completed his primary education and his preliminary Islamic studies. In 1332/1953, he departed for Qum to continue his study of the Islamic sciences, studying under the professors and teachers of the religious institution, including the main authorities in jurisprudence (*maraji'*).

In 1341/1962, he became a collaborator of *Maktab-i-Islam*, a religious and scientific journal, writing a series of articles on Islamic ethics. Thee articles were later collected into a book published under the title *Ethical and Psychological Problems*. Nine editions of the Persian original of this book have been published, and it has also been translated into Arabic and, most recently, English.

In 1342/1963, he travelled to Germany for medical treatment, and returning to Iran after a stay of several months, he wrote a book called *The Face of Western Civilization*. The book includes a comparative discussion of Western and Islamic civilization, and in it, the author seeks to prove, by way of a comprehensive, reasoned, and exact comparison, the superiority of the comprehensive and multi-dimensional civilization of Islam to that of the West. This book has recently been reprinted for the seventh time. In 1349/1970, it was translated into English by a British Orientalist, F. G. Goulding, and it aroused much attention in Europe. Articles concerning the book appeared in several Western periodicals, and the BBC arranged an interview with the translator in which the reasons for translating the book and the reception accorded it in England were discussed. The English version of the book has up to now been printed three times in England, five times in Iran, and twice in America.

About three years after the publication of the English translation, Rudolf Singler, a German university professor, translated it into German, and the version he produced proved influential in Germany. One of the leaders of the Social Democratic Party informed the translator in a letter that the book had left a profound impression upon him, causing him to change his views of Islam, and that he would recommend the book to his friends. The German translation has now been reprinted three times.

The English and German versions of the book were reprinted by the Ministry of Islamic Guidance for wide distribution abroad through the Ministry of Foreign Affairs and the Islamic Students' Associations abroad.

At the same time that the first printing of the German translation was published, an Indian Muslim scholar by the name of Maulana Raushan Ali translated it into Urdu for distribution in India and Pakistan. This Urdu translation has now been reprinted five times.

Sayyid Mujtaba Musavi Lari has also written a pamphlet on *tauhid* (divine unity), which was translated in England and published several times in America.

In 1343/1964, he established a charitable organization in Lar with the purposes of propagating Islam, teaching Islam to rural youth, and helping the needy. This organization remained active until 1346/1967. Its main accomplishments were the dispatch of students of the religious sciences to the countryside to teach Islam to children and young people; providing thousands of school children with clothing, books and writing equipment; building a number of mosques, schools, and clinics in towns and villages; and the provision of miscellaneous services.

Sayyid Mujtaba Musavi Lari pursued his interest in Islamic ethics, writing new articles on the subject. In 1353/1974, a collection of these articles, revised and supplemented, appeared in book form under the title, *The Function of Ethics in Human Development.* This book has now been reprinted six times.

In 1357/1978, he travelled to America at the invitation of an Islamic organization in that country. He then went to England and France and after returning to Iran began writing a series of articles on Islamic ideology for the magazine *Soroush.* These articles were later collected in a four-volume book on the fundamental beliefs of Islam (*tauhid,* divine justice, prophethood, imamate, and resurrection) under the title *The Foundations of Islamic Doctrine.*

This four-volume work has been translated into Arabic, some parts of it having already been printed three times. The English translation of the first volume of this work forms the present book; the remaining volumes will also be translated and published. Urdu, Hindi and French translations are also underway; two volumes of the French translation have already appeared.

In 1359/1980, Sayyid Mujtaba Musavi Lari established an organization in Qum called Office for the Diffusion of Islamic Culture Abroad. It dispatches free copes of his translated works to interested persons throughout the world. It has also undertaken the printing of a Quran for free distribution among Muslim individuals, institutions and religious schools in Africa.

In the Name of God, Most Gracious, Most Merciful

Lesson One
Prophethood

Acquaintance with the School of the Prophets

In the world where our existence unfolds, we have never heard of or seen an organization or administration that is left to its own devices without a supervisor being responsible for it. Human reason and intelligence cannot accept that social institutions be without a leader or ruler, and no thinker will approve of an organizational formula that lacks a responsible leader.

Given that reason and logic emphasize the necessity of a responsible leader for even the smallest social unit, how can humanity as a whole attain the basic goals to which it aspires or acquire the lofty values of which it is worthy, without a leader and chief?

Now the Creator, within the system of creation, has not withheld anything that may be needed for any being to advance and attain a fitting degree of perfection; He has placed the necessary means and tools at the disposal of all things, and given to each part of every animate being and plant exactly what it needs. How then can it be believed that in the system of legislating for the human being He should overlook the sending of Prophets who play such a sensitive and multifaceted role in the evolution of the human being, or that He should remain indifferent to this fundamental pillar?

Furthermore, can any intelligent person accept that the vast scheme of being, with all the wonder-inducing manifestations of life, should be based on aimlessness and purposelessness? Is it possible to attribute such an irrational act to the sublime Creator? The question of reward and punishment, in a precise and calculated form, is involved here.

It is an indubitable scientific principle that purposiveness is the concomitant of all life, thought and will. It is not possible that a wise being should consciously undertake an action in which no goal or purpose resides.

Apart from the fact that the human being instinctively regards an aimless act as incompatible with wisdom and intelligence, he can clearly perceive that all the atoms in the world of being are ruled by order and calculation. So just as the orderliness of life springs from the knowledge and wisdom of the Creator, the same may be said of the purposiveness of the whole scheme of being, including the existence of the human being.

Is God indifferent to the fate of humans? Has He abandoned them to their own devices, so they may shed each other's blood, commit any crime they like, and transform the world into a fiery hell?

A God Who holds back nothing in order for every creature to attain its perfection cannot possibly be indifferent to the human being's attaining the degree of perfection suitable to him. On the contrary, just as He guides the human being to material perfection by means of his instincts, He guides him to his true perfection both by means of the innate guidance of his nature and by means of legislative guidance, for innate guidance needs help when confronting the instincts.

The Quran says: "*We will give help to both groups, those who worship the world and those who seek the hereafter, so that none should remain deprived of the favor and generosity of their Lord.*"(17:18)

If the human being were left alone in the world with his own hopes, everyone would judge on the basis of his own temperament and taste. He would do whatever he found pleasing and conformable to his inclinations. Every individual would follow his own path in order to secure his interests, and the result would be a clash of desires and interests, leading to the severance of individual and social relations and unending corruption and anarchy.

The French scholar, Emile Dermenghem, writes in his book *The Life of Muhammad*: The Prophets are just as necessary for the world as the beneficial and wondrous forces of nature, such as the sun, rainfall, winter storms, which shake and cleave open dry and infertile land, covering them with freshness and verdure. The grandeur and legitimacy of such events can be deduced from their results: inward capacities that have received strength and confidence, hearts that have been given tranquility, wills that have been strengthened, tumults that have been quietened, moral diseases that have been cured, and finally, the supplications that have mounted up to heaven.[1]

It can be deduced from the Quran that one of the missions of the Prophets is ending differences among human beings and purifying them. The Quran says: "*Human beings were one community. God sent Messengers to give glad tidings to the good and a warning to the bad. He sent the Book in truth so they might judge justly in their disputes.*" (2:213)"*He it is Who sent a great Messenger among the unlettered Arabs, one from among them, who might recite to them the verses of God's revelation, purify them from the filth of ignorance and evil characteristics, and teach them the Law contained in His Book, whereas previously they had been in the abyss of ignorance and misguidance.*" (62:2)"*O Lord, make our offspring worthy of Your raising Messengers from among them who will recite Your verses to human beings, who will teach them the knowledge of the Book and wisdom, and cleanse and purify their souls from all ignorance and ugliness.*" (2:128)

The Prophets came in order to convey to human beings Divine knowledge, free of all forms of illusion and error. They came to proclaim to the human being a series of truths which a person would never have attained unaided, such as matters lying beyond the natural realm like death, the intermediate realm, and resurrection.

In Divine schools of thought, the mode of thought that underlies both belief and action, the knowledge of the material and spiritual dimensions of human existence, lies within the bounds of the human being's capacity to perceive. For the human being approaches true happiness, and his growth and ascent become possible, only when his constant and fundamental needs are recognized, preserved and satisfied in a balanced fashion.

One of the most fundamental missions of the Prophets, is, then, to bring the excesses of that which causes the human being trouble and torment in his rebellious spirit, under control and reduce them to order, so as to pacify its rebellious tendencies. Thus we see that in the school of the Prophets, pleasures are not negated nor is their value and essentiality denied.

The supreme ideal of the Prophets, who are the source of virtue and the gushing springs of human ethics, is to cure and nurture the human spirit in such a way that it reaches a higher truth and ascends toward ethical values. Through the realistic and perceptive training the human being receives from the Prophets, he advances on a path that leads to infinity and he distances himself from alienation. It is natural that those who establish such a program of action should have been chosen at the threshold of heavenly power, the power of One Who is aware of all the mysteries of the human being's creation and the needs of his soul.

The selection that takes place with respect to the Prophets is based on the ascertainment of an individual's being as a complete model of the powers and faculties of the human being. In order to ascend existentially, to cure their souls and to attain the heavenly rank of fruition, human beings must enter the sphere of the teachings of the Prophets; it is only then that their humanity can be fully realized.

The valuable element that the human being represents in this world has not been abandoned or left to its own devices, nor has God wished to entrust the destiny of the human being to capricious oppressors who sinking their poisonous claws into the spirit and mind of the human being begin their exploitation of humanity by exploiting its mind. For then mankind would be held back from true advancement and be impelled in the direction of false and valueless aims.

Since intellectual and creedal criteria have always played a determining role and constitute an extremely effective factor in the shaping of life, the Prophets have always commenced their mission in precisely this area. Because the intellectual criteria of society are generally tainted by the ignorance of Divine guidance, they have abolished those criteria and presented new, positive and fruitful criteria to replace them.

The Prophets are, then, the true revolutionaries of history. Shining forth in the darkness, they have come forth to struggle against the sources of corrupt belief and misguidance, and to guide the most sacred and beautiful manifestation of the human spirit to its true and proper course. They rescue the human being from shameful forms of worship that are not worthy of his lofty station, and hold him back from all forms of erroneous thought and deviance that arise in his search for God and inflict harm on him. They conduct him from the confines of ignorance to the region of light and perception, because all the paths of true happiness and salvation lead to the assertion of God's oneness.

At the same time, the Prophets guarantee the freedom of the human being in accepting belief; he is free to exercise his will by accepting either unbelief or belief. The Quran says: *"O Prophet, say: the religion of truth is that which has come unto you from your Lord. So let whoever wishes believe, and whoever wishes, be an unbeliever."* (18:29)The Quran explicitly rejects the imposition of belief by saying: *"There is no coercion or compulsion in the acceptance of religion."* (2:256)

If we examine deeply the content of the teachings to the Prophets, which determine the method to be followed by all true movements of reform and liberation, we will see that their sole aim was guiding human beings to felicity.

Because God looks upon His servants with favor, He chooses as Prophets the most perfect of human beings, who first enter the arena of human thought and belief, creating there a vast outpouring of energy, and then enter the sphere of action and ethics, in order to draw human beings's attention away from the natural realm to that which lies beyond nature. Thereby they liberate the human being from the scandalous and demeaning multiplicity of gods and from infatuation with the world and material phenomena. They cleanse their minds and their hearts and attach them to a source of hope and mercy that bestows tranquility on their souls.

Once the human being recognizes the origin of his creation and believes in the unseen forces of the world that lies beyond the natural realm, he learns a program of advancement toward perfection from the guides on the path to truth, the chosen ones of the Divine threshold. For it is they who demonstrate to human society its origin and the goal of perfection toward which it must strive. The human being, then, begins his efforts to reach God, for it is this that is the lofty goal of all being, and he addresses his Lord as follows: *"We have heard Your command and obey it, O Lord; we seek your forgiveness and know that our movement is toward You."* (2:285)

The Commander of the Faithful, Ali, upon whom be peace, says: "God sent the Prophets to remove the veils covering the human being's innate nature and to bring forth the treasures of thought hidden within him."[2] He also says in the first Sermon of the *Nahj al-Balaghah*: "God Almighty raised Prophets from among the sons of Adam and took from them a covenant that they would propagate His message. This was after most human beings had perverted the Divine covenant, becoming ignorant of God, the supreme truth, and assigning likenesses to Him, and after Satan had turned them away from the course of innate nature and disposition, preventing them from worshipping God.

"It was then that the Creator sent them a succession of Prophets, to remind them of the bounties that they had forgotten and to demand of them that they fulfil their primordial covenant with God, and to make manifest the hidden treasures and resplendent signs that the hand of Divine power and destiny had placed within them. "

The school of thought established by the Prophets contains a specific view of the world and society which sets human thought on a distinctive course. Without doubt, the human being's interpretation of the world and the realities of life is a factor which determines a broad area of his efforts and activities.

The first lesson taught by heavenly religions and their most fundamental pillar consists of the Divine unity. At the beginning of their missions, the Prophets raised the cry of Divine unity, seeking thereby to liberate human thought from the bondage of illusion and humiliating subjection to false and mendacious divinities. Within a short period, they conveyed their Divine message to all classes of society in their age—human beings and women, the old and the young, the rulers and the powerful. They strove to sever the bonds of servitude and to rend the veils of ignorance that were obscuring the mind and intellect of the human being. Through monotheism, they sought to advance society and cleanse the spirit of all peoples from the contamination of everything other than God.

Unlike the philosophers, the Messengers of God did not content themselves with training human beings' minds. Their efforts to convey the message of God's unity also penetrated human beings' hearts, and after cleansing their intellects, they filled the dwelling of the heart with that true love which is a necessary consequence of the human being's spiritual ascent. It is this veritable love which impels human beings towards dynamic and passionate motion, and makes of them vibrant and creative personalities. Passionate love for the infinite source of existence is like the motor for human life; if it be taken away from the human being, he becomes a lifeless and motionless form.

The principle of Divine unity distinguishes the structure of the society in which it prevails from all other societies, with respect to both its internal and its external relationships; it creates a profound structural change in whatever society accepts it, to such a degree that in its ability to reform both the individual and society, no other movement in human history can be compared with it. In addition to the fact that it clarifies the relationship of the human being with the source of being, through restricting all worship to the Creator of the world Who is the absolute ruler and owner of all things, it also determines economic, political and legal relationships among human beings.

The word "mission" (*ba'that*) is used in Islamic texts to designate the function of the Prophets, a word that contains the sense of an outpouring of energy, swiftness in action, and unrelenting effort. No better or more precise word could be found to designate the profound and fundamental movement that is that of the Prophets.

The unity of sovereignty derives from the oneness of the Creator, because the sole authority for the fashioning of laws and the issuing of commands is His unique essence. It is the exclusive right of the Creator of being to command and prohibit, and for this reason the doctrine of Divine unity necessarily implies that none other than God has the right to exercise sovereign power or promulgate laws.

A full understanding of Divine unity goes beyond the recognition that the world has only one Creator; we must also recognize that it has only one sovereign and only one legislator, and that precisely this concept brings to an end the tyranny of oppressive and arbitrary rulers.

Whoever claims to possess sovereignty and the powers that flow from it has, in reality, claimed divinity, for one of the indications of polytheism is for the human being to imagine that he possesses sovereignty and an unconditional right to legislate.. This contradicts the Divine unity and the fundamental beliefs of religion. It is a basic mission and concern of heavenly religions that they propagate the true meaning of the Divine unity in order to deliver the masses of humanity and save them, by their belief in the oneness of God, from slavery to unjust and arbitrary rule.

If it were not for the remarkable profundity and comprehensiveness exhibited by the contents of religion, and if it were not for the purposive movement of the Prophets, and their summons to awareness and perception, the conditions of human societies would never have changed. Today there would be no trace of humanity left, and we would have no path to convey us to the station of true love.

In the course of human history, it is only religion with its comprehensiveness and all-inclusive scope that has been able to come to the aid of human beings, to lead the masses by the hand, and play the most crucial of roles in guiding them toward ascent and advancement.

No dimension of human existence has remained untouched by the positive effect of the Prophets, and their influence even on the formation and growth of human knowledge has been very extensive. If we examine the history of the missions of the Prophets and the swift, remarkable and unparalleled growth of their movements, we will see that more than anyone else, they have served as sources of profound intellectual change and transformation in society. It is they who have breathed into the form of humanity the spirit of brotherhood, love and philanthropy, and who have taught human beings the culture of justice, peace and unity.

God has attributed to Himself the reconciliation of hearts and the establishment of solidarity that occurred as a result of Islam and the efforts of the Noble Prophet: *"He is the God Who has reinforced you with His own aid and the assistance of the believers, and joined their hearts together. Were you to spend all the riches in the world thus to unite and reconcile them, you would be unable to do so. Rather, it is God Who has joined their hearts together for He is empowered over all things and all-knowing of the mysteries and benefits contained in all things."* (8:66)

The Prophet David was able to establish the most just of all conceivable judicial and political structures on the basis of the Divine message he had received. The Quran says: *"O David, We have bestowed rule on earth upon you, so rule justly among human beings. Never follow your own inclinations, for this will lead you away from God's path. Those who stray from God's path will be chastised with a great punishment, for they have forgotten the day of reckoning."* (38:26)

The celebrated historian, Will Durant, says: "Religion bestows a profound and masterly power and capacity on both society and the state. The rites and practices of religion give tranquility to the spirit, link the generations together, and bind individuals to each other, thus strengthening the fabric of society."[3]

If such a Divine movement had not taken place in human history, mankind would have been eternally entangled in the swamp of misguidance and humiliation and could never have entered the realm of virtue and perfection. Even those individuals who deny the Prophets have benefited in some way from the blessed legacy of those human beings of God, from the great cultural achievements they brought about which wrought transformations and fashioned history.

Furthermore, there is a profound and absolute link between the movement of the Prophets and knowledge in the absolute sense. Those periods in which historical movements were led by human beings of God were among the most brilliant epochs of human history with respect to scientific advancement.

The authentic teachings of Divine schools of thought, together with the foundations and principles they expounded, laid both a theoretical and a practical groundwork for appropriate social relations that permit the sciences to advance. Numerous are those philosophers and scientists throughout the world whose profound insights have been inspired in them by the Prophets, those guides to Divine unity.

Lesson Two
To whom belongs the right to legislate?

Consider the thinking element within the human being and the relatively high degree of intellectual power it has gradually come to attain since the beginning of the human being's existence on earth. Examine, too, his capacities and his incapacities, and the problems and hardships with which he is faced. Despite all his faculties and properties, has he ever been able, or is he now able, to advance on a straight path of perfection merely by relying on his own mind? Can he preserve himself from all deviation and decline, or put an end to the disorders that plague his existence? Can he plant the sapling of virtue and piety in the soil of his own being, alone and without drawing on the guidance of the teachers whom heaven has sent? Can he, unaided, bring to fruition the talents and capacities that are latent within him? If until now he has been unable to do any of these things, to implement any of these ideals, it is certain that he will be unable to do so in the future either.

Although some of his capacities may increase in the future, we must also accept that the difficulties and problems with which he is faced will also increase and grow more complex, just as his present problems are greater than those that confronted him in the past.

Apart from this, the scope of the intellect's ability to perceive and to judge is a limited area which is illuminated only by the light of knowledge and learning. What lies beyond reason is enveloped in veils of obscurity and darkness and lies beyond the grasp of our minds. By contrast, a considerable part of the teachings of God's Messengers relates precisely to the realities of which we are ignorant and unaware; it consists of the exposition of truths that are not contained within the sphere of our external perception.

In order to become acquainted as much as possible with the origin of all beings, with the duties of the human being and other realities, we need a teacher and a guide sent by God, who will guide us toward perfection and the aim of creation with teachings that are both clear and comprehensive. This is possible only by means of revelation and the teachings of Prophets who have a direct relationship with the source of creation and the lamp of whose intellects has been kindled from the eternal flame of His infinite knowledge.

Another portion of the Prophets' teachings relates to the reform of our state and the correction of the errors into which we have fallen. Whenever the sphere of what is knowable to us is penetrated by mistake or error, it is possible to correct the error and make up for the deficiency in our knowledge by referring to the guidance of the Prophets. We will thus be able to travel on a path that we could never traverse without the aid of those guides.

Thus we come to understand the significance and value of the mission of the Prophets and the services rendered by them in guiding the human beings and elevating them to the pinnacle of triumph and perfection.

We know that the human being attains and develops his knowledge gradually. If science wishes to display to the human being the principles of his development, it must first be acquainted with all of his powers, capacities, and inner mysteries, and discern all of his various needs. In the opinion of all contemporary thinkers who count as authorities in the areas of education, sociology and politics, any plan or ideology that fails to take into account the basic nature of the human being is bound to be fruitless and valueless.

The establishment of laws is dependent not only on a complete knowledge of all the dimensions of human existence but also on a knowledge of the other beings with which the human being has dealings. It also requires a knowledge of society and its complex relationships. Furthermore, the legislator must be completely removed from distorting and misguiding factors such as ambition, selfishness, personal inclination and desire, which militate against the acquisition of perfect knowledge. It is factors and obstacles such as these which cause the human beings to differ in their assessment of good and evil and the definition and implementation of justice.

Is it possible to cure a sick person without diagnosing his illness? Establishing laws for the human being without understanding his essence and permitting it to remain covered in a host of unknowns, is exactly like trying to cure a patient whose illness is unknown.

For this reason, and because no school of thought has yet succeeded in defining the human being, any plan in the area of legislation is bound to end in failure and defeat.

Despite all the efforts that have been made to discover the secrets contained in the existence of the human being (who is only one small entity among the countless and varied beings found in the scheme of the universe), and despite all the researches carried out by scientific associations having at their disposal precise and complex instruments—despite all this, who can doubt that there are numerous unconquered peaks in the spiritual being and inner world of the human being that we have not even glimpsed?

It is possible that a person may know many scientific and technical facts but be completely ignorant of one topic—namely, the limits and nature of his own being. The knowledge he has acquired is next to zero when compared to this ignorance. Ignorance of the limited nature of one's ability to perceive and understand gives rise to many other forms of ignorance; it causes the human being to turn his back on many truths and avert his gaze from many realities.

If all obscure points concerning the corporeal aspect of the human being had been clarified, the scientific researches carried out throughout the world by millions of scientists would still be in vain. A French scholar says: "However much we try, we cannot render these mechanisms comprehensible to our minds. All we know is that the regularity of the parts of our body is greater and more precise than that of a thousand great machines operated by the most highly specialized engineers.

"If you do not regard our opinion as a kind of belittlement or insult, all doctors and specialists who exert themselves in their field are convinced that the knowledge we have acquired until now is paltry and insignificant when compared to what we need to know in the future. The truth is that the human being is a complex, obscure and indivisible whole that cannot easily be known. We still lack the methods that would enable us to know him in all of his different parts and, as a whole, as well as in his relations with his environment. Numerous techniques and precise sciences would be needed for such an undertaking, and each science would be able to study only one part of the complex system that is the human being, yielding only a partial result. We advance on this path only so far as technological progress permits us, and the totality of the abstract concepts we acquire does not furnish us a perception of the reality of the human being, for there are numerous significant and valuable points that remain unclarified. Anatomy, physiology, chemistry, education, history, economics, together with all their branches, cannot reach the ground of the human being's essence."[4]

With respect to the astonishing activities of his soul, human being is without doubt a deep and limitless ocean, and our worldly knowledge concerning him is inevitably slight and insignificant. Who can claim to have discovered all the capacities and minutiae contained within this mysterious being, or to be aware of all his capacities and the degrees of perfection that are open to him? Thus we conclude that we have but a drop of insignificant knowledge, shot through with doubt and hesitation, compared tc an ocean of ignorance and unknowing.

Science today is then confronted with the problem of the limitation of human powers, on the one hand, and the expanse and infiniteness of the world and of the human being, on the other; this problem has induced both bewilderment and humility in science. In fact, science itself has aided us in understanding that the knowledge of the human being can illumine only a small and insignificant part of this expansive world.

Now let us see whether science and intellect alone can assume the mission of impelling the human being to perfection. A world that cannot provide a precise knowledge of being, that does not know what the human being is, from the point of view of either body or soul, that is ignorant of the mysterious social relationships that arise from his spiritual and bodily properties—does such a world have the capacity to lay down laws for the human being that will reflect intelligence and wisdom, and be formed in accordance with the knowledge of the human being's true needs in their various dimensions? Laws that will ensure his true happiness, answer the totality of his needs, and enable him to walk on the path that benefits him?

As long as we do not know what we wish to make, and for what purpose and for whose sake, how can we even speak of laying down a plan and a program? Those schools of thought which claim to be able to make the human being's capacities blossom do so without first knowing what the human being is. How can they succeed in turning him into a being that would deserve all those efforts? The human being's basic problem today is not simply the acquisition of power but rather which of the various roads laid out before him he should travel.

Many scientific topics and principles were accepted unanimously by thinkers of the past, but with the passage of time and the advancement of knowledge it has become apparent that their views were erroneous and invalid.

If we look at the history of legislation among the nations of the world, we will see that many laws which were the product of careful reflection and lengthy study on the part of outstanding experts and were drawn up with recourse to considerable scientific and intellectual resources, were proved mistaken and inadequate by the passage of time and by the emergence of more accurate research. That the social utility of which was yesterday regarded as proven is seen today as palpably inappropriate and even harmful. The place of such laws is then taken by a new set of laws which will, in turn, be amended and revised in accordance with the advancement of science and thought.

Naturally this does not mean that all the regulations and ordinances that originate in the human mind are useless and incorrect. The point is that because of such errors and their lack of inerrancy, man-made legal systems are incapable of providing for the different needs of the human beings and of leading society. It is entirely true that some scholars have expressed valuable views on the subject of legislation, but their ideas and works have been influenced, directly and indirectly, by the teachings of the Prophets.

We can clearly see that deficiency and inadequacy are the hallmark of all those systems in the world that derive from man-made laws. Moral and material inadequacy, forms of corruption that kill the personality of the human being and drag him down to decline—all these are caused by regulations and laws that derive from human thought. The insufficiency and fallibility of human laws is sufficient proof of this.

Even if they acquire knowledge of the principles of human development, science and human thought are unable to assume alone the responsibility for the human being's ascent. Such a mission presupposes freedom from arbitrary and capricious desire and from the desire for advantage, for these are factors which prevent the human being from realizing his knowledge of self.

The human being's love of the self and his devotion to its interests, as well as to whatever stands in relationship to him, is so profound that on a broad scale, whether consciously or unconsciously, he looks at all things from the point of view of his own interests; self-love deprives him of true realism. When taken to the extreme, the pursuit of self-interest becomes a powerful and destructive factor that does away with the human being's honor. A condition appears in the human being such that every instant he is planning the violation of ethical norms and transgression against the rights of others, in order to draw to himself all conceivable benefits and gains. There is thus no guarantee that the human being can analyze affairs with true impartiality and establish just laws.

Are those who have studied the human being and then—whether individually or collectively—established legal system, really aware of the problem and its solution? Have they avoided the trap of egoism, and are their thoughts and reflections immune from self-interest, discrimination and error? Are they truly aware of the problems of groups and classes other than their own, scattered across the world, and the solutions those problems call for? Are they fully protected from the arbitrary whims and desires, the threats and the tricks, of the wielders of power and influence, of biased and evil-hearted the human beings?

Given all of these questions, it is possible to hope that such founders of legal systems will prove to be ideal, positive and desirable elements? Finally, is it confidently possible to ensure the happiness of the human being by following and submitting to such dubious systems?

Now all these systems are supposed to bring order and equilibrium to the capacities and abilities of the human being, to his perception and choice; they are situated on a higher level than he is. How, then, can it be logically correct that the human being, the intended object of this process, should also be its subject? The human being, the object of the process, wishes to establish a system that will bring order and equilibrium, but ought not he himself be situated within four impenetrable walls that cannot be reached by the factors of deviance and error? If this is necessary, how is to be achieved?

Do the vision, perception and other faculties of the human being extend far enough to permit him to assume a position for which he is not qualified, to establish laws and regulations that take into account the different dimensions of the human being and bring order into all the affairs of the individual and of society, and solve both present difficulties and future problems?

Objective realities without doubt lead us to conclude that the human being is incapable of truly knowing his own individual world or the world of being, and that, at the same time, he faces obscure, complex and vital problems that call for solution.

It is here that the inability of science and thought to fulfil such a mission becomes fully apparent. Even if the ray of science were able one day to illumine all the corners of human existence and to solve all those mysteries that were thought incapable of solution, it would still be unable to guarantee human happiness, given the fact that the human being is by nature condemned to live beneath the sway of self-interest and personal inclination.

Another problem that arises with respect to human legislation concerns the difference in levels of education and cultural circumstances prevailing among individuals that belong to different ranks of society. Judgements, interpretations and assessments of existing realities, as well as of national concepts and customs and many other matters, will differ according to the educational, cultural and social situation in which an individual has grown up. Even the viewpoint of a single class in society is not uniform; the ways in which members of that class elaborate concepts and interpret certain words and terms may be completely different from each other.

Think of all the different interpretations of words such as peace, justice and equality, and of how the interpretation made by every individual or group corresponds to his breadth of vision or thought, as well as to personal or collective viewpoints. Normal people understand these truths in a clear and humane sense, but the rulers and leaders of society look on these terms and the matters connected with them in quite a different way.

Without doubt, the influence on the human beings of their environment is an important factor contributing to the deficiency and inadequacy of man-made laws. Legal scholars and legislators, subject to the influence of the ideas and beliefs prevailing in their societies, accept as irrefutable truth whatever they absorb from their environment. When they draw up laws, their minds are drawn, consciously or unconsciously, to the beliefs and ideas they have acquired or inherited. The specific cultural atmosphere of society robs them of a realistic spirit and does not permit them to perceive realities as they truly are.

Further, the views and opinions of the human being change according to different situations and conditions; as a result of the transformations, events and advances that occur in his life, his views and positions will change.

Once a the human being is installed in the seat of power, his ideas and manner of judgment will no longer be the same as when he was an ordinary individual without any power. According to circumstances, he will look at things in two quite different ways. Once a the human being's position changes, his views may be so thoroughly transformed that they no longer bear any resemblance to those he held in the past or have any connection with them; it is as if everything has taken on a new meaning for him.

This is an obvious reality; everyone has seen in his own lifetime examples of these changes in direction as individuals rise and fall in the course of their lives. In addition, when drawing up laws, legislators generally take into account the desires and wishes of the majority, not the truth, even though those desires and wishes may not be beneficial and even be harmful for the individual and for society.

Addressing himself to the inadequacies of these various schools of thought that turn out to be opposed to the advancement and welfare of mankind, Rousseau makes the following realistic remarks: "In order to discover the best possible laws that should truly benefit all nations, a universal intelligence is needed that should be aware of all human passions but not experience them itself; that should have no connection with nature but know it intimately; and whose happiness is not in any way dependent on us but is willing to help us in attaining our happiness."[5]

Another thinker says: "All of the different systems of government that have been fashioned by the thoughts and ideas of theoreticians are mere castles in the sky. Both the the human being who was the good of the French Revolution and the the human being who, according to the vision of Marx and Lenin, is to build the society of the future, are unreal. Let us not forget that the laws governing the relations of the human beings with each other have not yet been discovered. Both physiology and economics are imperfect sciences, or even pseudo-sciences. It thus appears that the environment we have created around ourselves with the aid of science is not worthy of us, because it has been created in a haphazard way, without adequate knowledge of the human being's nature or attention to his nature."[6]

Legislation can belong, then, only to God, Whose knowledge embraces all directions and dimensions. He knows the human being and his relations with the world and other beings; He is aware of the changes and developments that occur in the human being and the world; He has infinite knowledge of the conditions to which the human being is subject and the limits of his perfection; and His essence is exalted above all the factors that hold the human being back and inflict harm on him. The Quran says: *"The One Who created, does He not know?"* (67:14)

Lesson Three
A Rich and Fruitful School of Thought

The first condition for attaining the true goals of life, the lofty rank of happiness, and, not least, a comprehensive and authentic sys-tem of governance, is to appreciate, in a precise and scientific way, the necessity for a message and a Messenger. This recognition will enable us to conquer new horizons and journey toward undiscovered and virgin territories of human thought.

The human being has extensive resources at his disposal and he may enter a network of guidance, both within his own being and within the world where he lives, through the laws that God has laid down for him. That guidance is protected against all deviation and error, and its bearer is preserved, through the inerrancy bestowed on him by the Creator, from all sin, error, and forgetfulness in the receipt, promulgation and implementation of revelation. Therefore, for those who draw their inspiration from sound thought, no doubt will remain that a system based on such guidance is able to secure the true interests, moral and material, of mankind.

The efforts of the Prophets in their summons to the human beings are directed to giving shape to God's rule over mankind, this being the most just form of rule conceivable. In such a system, the domination of the human being over the human being and his imprisonment in the grasp of demonic oppressors will be fully negated. The intrinsic value and force of the words of the Prophet derive from the fact that he is the bearer of God's message.

The knowledge of the true human being and of human reality forms the basis of the worldview and the planning of all Divine schools of thought. A school of thought that is based on the very creation of the human being, that is aware of all the dimensions of his existence, and that supervises with infinite knowledge all of his natural properties, is well able, in the course of its planning and elaboration of laws, to take into account all the fundamental and authentic concerns of the human being.

Setting itself against all ego worship, all desire for fame, all search for mastery over the powers of nature, the movement of the Prophets derives its substance from the Divine will; it is God Who is the source of their actions. If the Prophets come into conflict with the human beings, it is fundamentally because of the limited ideas of the human beings; the Prophets attempt to bring to an end the narrow and limited vision of the human beings and to introduce them to a more productive mode of thought.

The distinctive feature of the system of governance established by the Prophets is the realization of justice in the true and comprehensive sense of the word. By virtue of the principles underlying the movement of the Prophets, the most just social relations come into existence in a way that edifies the human being's inner being. The equality of the human beings on a basis of brotherhood is translated into reality. It is therefore impossible to ensure social justice in the true meaning except by way of God's message.

At the same time, the schools of thought established by the Prophets give positive answer to the human being's profoundly felt need for freedom, and thereby break all the inner chains that fetter the human being's capacities, energies and will, and transform his vitality into stagnation. Parallel to this inner liberation of the human being, the Prophets also endow his outer life with freedom, setting him free from servitude to the tyrants of his age.

Under such conditions, there is no longer any question of laying down laws that are inadequate and erroneous, nor of rulers coercively enforcing their arbitrary will. For then, the legislator is God, God Who has created the world and all its inhabitants and knows in a precise and perfect fashion how to meet all the needs of the human beings in their various dimensions.

Similarly, there is no question of ignorance or imperfect knowledge or of the slightest degree of oppression and injustice; selfishness and self-interest do not exist. These are realities that deserve our deepest attention, and we must recognize the objective effect of all those ordinances which God has promulgated for the sake of social life and the resurrection of the human being. The Quran says: "*Who can rule better than God?*" (5:55) "*God it is Who determines our social relations and rules over our deeds and conduct; He is the best of all rulers.*" (7:87) "*Do they desire the rule of ignorance, whereas there is no ruler better than God?*" (5:50)

One of the distinguishing characteristics of the school of thought founded by the Prophets is that according to their teachings, the interests of society also benefit the interests of the individual, because the life of the human being never terminates, his interests being ensured by a long line that continued after his death.

Wherever the laws of heaven make their appearance and a prophetic mission, appearing as a Divine phenomenon, takes on the responsibility of responding to the intellectual, spiritual and material needs of the human being, as well as reforming both the individual and society—wherever this occurs, nothing will be reflected but reality. With respect to God, the question of environmental conditions and susceptibility to the concepts prevailing in society and culture does not even arise; there is also no question of the effect of change giving thought a new direction. The factors that cause the human being to lose faith in his ability to attain the truth and perceive his true interests are thus totally negated.

In the Divine school of thought, it is faith, the symbol of the human being's intellectual ascent, which functions as a powerful support for ensuring the implementation of the law. This is another advantage of systems of governance based on religion, as well as being a gushing spring from which the reality of existence flows forth.

In societies that are founded by Prophets, the human being is commonly entrusted with the supervision of his own person; he relies on his own findings, acquisitions and efforts. At the same time that the human being is thus free, he feels an intense sense of responsibility toward God. He measures every act he wishes to undertake and every position he wishes to take up against the criteria of religion, and then personally assumes the responsibility for that act and position. He knows that to act on the basis of duty will bring numerous fruitful results, and that if he turns his back on his duties, he must be ready to face harmful effects and to endure evil consequences. A sense of duty vis-a-vis the Divine laws that embrace all dimensions of human life causes the human being to submit to the will of God with all of his being.

The training of the human being in the school of the Prophets takes place in such a way that gradually his passionate inclinations gradually yield to truly human and Divine desires, permitting him ultimately to rise to the glorious station of servitude to God and being His representative on earth, this being the true nature of the fully evolved the human being.

By contrast, in legal systems of human origin, where there is no question of religious belief in a legislator, law lacks moral underpinning and the ability to influence the human beings profoundly and comprehensively. Everyone is constantly thinking how he might best shake off the constraints of the law, with the result that the implementation of the law faces all kinds of difficulty. Various coercive forces must be broadly deployed in order to ensure it. If the law contradicts the desires of the people, the task of its implementation becomes particularly complex and difficult. When such a law is enforced, it will be met with a storm of anger, dislike and repulsion, and it is only pressure that can then impose it.

No Guarantee for the Implementation of Human Law

It is, of course, possible to find people in society who believe in and adhere to laws and regulations of human origin, but it must be affirmed that such individuals are extremely rare and form the exception. They certainly do not represent the average member of society and cannot be regarded as a principal support of the social order. The practical effectiveness of a conscience that is not guaranteed by religious faith or principle is, moreover, very slight when compared to effectiveness of religious beliefs.

It must, therefore, be accepted that this advantage deriving from the teachings of the Prophets is restricted to the heavenly religions. If the spirit of people is nurtured with faith in God and religious belief serves as a support for legal principles, law takes on a universal aspect, and its implementation is guaranteed to a degree superior to the ability of human laws to influence the human beings.

Since belief has its roots in the activity of the existential mechanism of the human being and since it plays a basic role in the structure of human personality, profoundly altering the conditions of the soul, the human being comes to believe in and adhere to the laws of religion not only with his brain but with the entirely of his being. The certainty that religion shines like a light in the depths of the human being's being, illumining it and warming it at the same time.

The impetus that religion can create in the human being cannot be found in any non-religious school of thought. Experience has shown that other schools of thought are unsuccessful in this respect, because it is religion alone that relies on the heart, and the more firmly rooted faith becomes in the heart, the more it will serve as a source of dynamic activity.

The human being witnesses today the elaboration and ratification of laws on the part of societies that officially recognize all the human beings, irrespective of racial, national, religious or geographical differences, as possessing certain rights and values. Nonetheless, although scientific advances have created today more suitable conditions for the acceptance of reality, the attitude of different groups to the laws that represent their own accomplishment is entirely negative and denies those laws any influence or value.

What people accept in theory they do not observe in fact. Whenever the law concerns them directly and their interests and desires are threatened, they will not hesitate to cross the boundaries of the law, to perform inhuman acts, and to engage in trickery and sabotage. It is obvious that the attitude of others towards laws of this nature will also not be one of positive acceptance.

This disregard for the value of the human being, this violation of law and the expansion of political struggle and conflict, the unhealthy economic rivalries of powerful states with most countries in the world, the tempestuous waves of social crisis and moral corruption—all this shows clearly how shaky and unfirm is the position of man-made laws, how slight are their influence and standing from the point of view of implementation, and how limited is the sphere of their rule.

A brief look at the manner in which the Universal Declaration of Human Rights has been observed and implemented suffices to show that the only effect this declaration has had consists of the celebration of festivals, and the delivery of empty, meaningless lectures.

If we follow, step by step, the development of religious ideas among the masses of humanity, will this not cause us to conclude that non-religious principles, which do not derive from exalted concepts, are weak and inadequate? Will it not bring us to believe firmly in the veracity and truthfulness of religious systems which are nurtured with the power and majesty of the Lord of all creation and the influence of whose culture and ideology on the entire cultural life of the human being becomes more fully known every day through the researches of thinkers?

We must look at results, at the fruits that different schools of thought have borne in human society. Is not the reason for the failure of human laws in ensuring the human being's progress and happiness not to be sought in their having remained ignorant of the true nature of the human being and their neglect of his real needs and creative abilities?

All of this serves to elucidate a single truth: that belief in the school of thought of the Prophets is a guarantor for the life of society, a support for all healthy relationships among the human beings, and a protector for the oppressed masses, and it has always bestowed the gift of freedom and brotherhood on mankind. Whatever society, group or system does not set its face on this path and does not respond affirmatively to the liberating summons of God's Messengers to a more elevated life, will never experience true prosperity and salvation.

The school of thought of the Prophets has provided penal laws for those persons who may exceptionally transgress against God's law. These laws weigh the offence carefully and specify a punishment corresponding to the degree of seriousness of the crime and take into consideration the situation of the criminal.

Lesson Four
Miracles: An Effective and Eloquent Proof

In the mission and summons of the Prophets, the human being's free will and choice are the first subject to attract our attention. If the human being had no share of free will and choice, he would never have any need of Prophets, he would travel along a predetermined path, advancing automatically.

Thus, in accepting the mission of the Prophets, we must necessarily accept also the freedom of the human being; otherwise, the fundamental themes in the mission of the Prophets could never be put forward, and it would not be possible to find any justification for their message, a message which, in reality, awakens the human beings who are asleep and transforms them into free and conscious beings, not torpid masses without will.

The general law of guidance is a universal law that covers the entirety of being. Given the insufficiency of the instinctual guidance the human being contains within himself, given the fact that his motion is not predetermined, given the various defects that negate the idea of reason being an adequate guide to perfection and happiness—given all this, it is necessary that the deficiency within the human being be made good, that the vacuum within him be filled.

Therefore, the scheme of creation lays open before the human being the path of prophethood which will enable him to reach his unchanging goal. With the tools and resources that he has at his disposal to acquire knowledge and consciousness, he can then discover, within the sphere laid out by the Prophets, precise, clear and infallible instructions for the attainment of happiness, and find answers to both his long-standing and increasing needs.

It is a fundamental principle that nobody's claim can be accepted without proof, particularly if it is a big and lofty claim. Then more decisive and convincing proofs must be offered for the claim being advanced.

Therefore, for those who have accepted the worldview based on Divine unity as the foundation for their beliefs and their mode of viewing the world, whenever someone claims a particular relationship with God, the importance of the matter necessitates that it be examined carefully. One must look for the properties and characteristics that are necessary in guides of humanity in order to be able to recognize a true Prophet.

Given the significance of the rank of prophethood, the great responsibility borne by the Prophets and the role of their message in determining the different concerns of human life, Prophets must be able to furnish a decisive proof for their claim to prophethood. The proof must be of such a nature that it could be obtained only by means of God's infinite power, of forces that lie beyond nature.

History bears witness that the Prophets came to show the path of salvation to the human being who had become empty, and to remove the great obstacles that were standing in the way of his intellectual development and his innate perceptions, causing him to become alienated from himself. Thus, the human being was enabled to find anew what he had lost, and the groundwork was laid for the establishment of justice, a society based on equity, and an environment conducive to spiritual advancement.

The fulfillment of such a commitment was without doubt dependent on the possession of great spiritual capacities. The Prophets had first to be armed with the weapon of miracles, which provided them with a decisive force for entering the arena and beginning their mission.

A miracle is a deed performed by a Prophet, by the will of God, in order to demonstrate the truth of his claim to prophethood. The proof that the miracle constitutes is without any doubt an indication of the Prophet's relationship with the source of revelation, the Creator of being.

For the one who claims to possess a mission from heaven, to have a message from God, and to be in contact with another world, must perform a deed that lies beyond the confines of nature, a deed that will serve as his letter of credentials from the Creator and confirm his claim to be in contact with revelation.

To prevent His servants from falling into the trap of false

claimants to prophethood, God has placed this blazing lamp, this decisive proof, in the hands of his envoys to mankind, so that the face of truth should never be obscured by veils of trickery and deceit. Just as the form of the entire scheme of being and the existence of all phenomena is a clear proof of the existence of God and His pre-eternal unity, the miracle is a clear and manifest proof of the relationship of the Prophet with the source of revelation. Religion cannot be interpreted correctly except with reference to revelation; all the topics dealt with by religion become meaningless and worthless once severed from revelation.

A Prophet who loudly claims prophethood for himself is, in reality, issuing the human beings with a challenge to enter the field of struggle against him with greater seriousness and energy than his, through mobilizing all their capacities and resources. But despite their desperate efforts, they get nowhere in their confrontation with him, and in their utter impotence they are obliged to surrender.

The miracle of the Prophet is by its very nature a demonstration of his connection with the source of all being and the world of revelation; its properties are such that it is impossible for the human beings who are not connected to the world beyond nature to confront or resist it, however much they expend of their powers and energies.

Hence the demonstration of prophethood depends on the performance of a deed that transcends the limits set by natural norms and common laws, and the performance of such a deed is not possible without the permission of the Creator. This provides a criterion for distinguishing the true from the false.

Naturally, the miracle differs from other phenomena in the world only from our point of view, not from the point of view of the One Who has precise and complete knowledge of all the causes of existence.

Generally speaking, the proof of prophethood was provided by miracles in areas that were in each age the object of special attention, so that those specialized in each area might know that the deed in question was beyond the limits of human capacity. This is the starting point for the task of the Prophets; by taking into account the human beings' level of intellectual development, they conquer broad horizons of human belief and swiftly attain their exalted goals.

Denial and Negation on the Basis of Pride

Those who regard miracles as something impossible and unacceptable should know that their incredulity arises from a superficial and simplistic view of things. Many events occur in the material world of which the human being knows the causes, but there are other events which the natural sciences are unable to interpret and explain. We should not, therefore, arrogantly deny everything the cause of which is unknown to us, relying on our slight knowledge.

The human being's error is to imagine that he knows everything; when he cannot penetrate the depths of a problem, he proceeds simply to deny it. However, it is beyond dispute that certain limits have been set to the reach of our thought, and however much farther the realm of human knowledge be extended, it will always remain limited. It is not wise to try and extend our own limited knowledge and laws to embrace the whole of infinite being. The instruments of our science will not have enough power or capacity to examine many matters, for causes and determining factors are not limited to those things of which we are aware.

The miracles of the Prophets remain covered by the overall order of creation; it is we who on account of the limited scope of our awareness, and the cessation of our thought-mechanisms at the boundaries of the supra-natural realm, are unable to penetrate the unknown and virgin territories of the universe.

From the point of view of time and place, being is infinite, and that segment of it which has been studied by the human being cannot in any way provide him with a complete idea of being. Why, then, should it be objectionable if our questions concerning the causes of the miracles wrought by the Prophets remain unanswered?

It is not possible to compare miracles with the extraordinary states attained by ascetics, because deeds such as theirs do not lie beyond the scope of human thought and inspection, instruction and practice; they inevitably yield certain results and they can be performed by others who pursue the same course. Moreover, since accomplishments such as these derive from the limited powers of the human being, they cannot be performed under all conditions and without the use of certain instruments.

Furthermore, the deeds of ascetics are in many cases a kind of frivolous entertainment; they do not play any positive, constructive role in human life nor do they bear any fruit worth speaking of. No one will regard the deeds of ascetics as miraculous or a proof of communication with God.

As for the deeds wrought by geniuses, they result from their possessing the power of thought, intelligence and mental calculation, from their awareness of a series of precise scientific mysteries, the deduction and application of which depends on knowledge of certain complex and precise principles. None of this has anything in common with miracles. Anyone who studies the rudiments of one of the sciences can, in principle, reach the same result as a genius; it is a matter of education and instruction. Scientific accomplishment is restricted to certain cases and it is open to contradiction by other, similar attainments. A miracle depends on revelation and derives from the infinite power of God; it does not stand in need of education and instruction nor is it subject to rivalry.

Jesus, upon whom be peace, began speaking while still in the cradle without any teacher or instructor having the least to do with it, and without it being contradicted by another supra-normal phenomenon.

Imam Sadiq, upon whom be peace, said: "God bestowed miracles on Prophets to serve as a clear proof of their truthfulness and veracity. He does not give such proof to anyone except his Messengers and His Proofs, so that the true claimant to a connection with God should be distinguishable from cunning tricksters."[7]

It is for this reason that even a supra-normal act cannot withstand the force of a miracle; it loses its illusory power on the field of battle and is condemned to inevitable defeat.

We must bear in mind that the miracle never violates the law of causality or destroys the norms of creation. However, the powerful God Who has created the order now observable in the scheme of being through the relations of causes with effects is not Himself bound or imprisoned by these causes. Since He is absolutely empowered over them, there is nothing to prevent Him from originating miracles through an unknown and mysterious chain of causes, beyond the ability of today's science to interpret an unknown even to geniuses among the human beings of learning.

Taking into consideration the finiteness of our knowledge, our instruments of measurement and our powers of assessment, it is possible that the human being will never come to grasp those mysterious causes which are controlled and willed by God. Nonetheless, those Divine norms which are unknown to us should not be imagined to be outside the sphere of the law of causality.

We have said that the miracles of the Prophets indicate a supranatural relationship; they arise from the manifestation of the light of Divine unity, and they are a part of the will of the Divine essence which has created all phenomena in the world and set universal schemes and unique laws and place to rule over them.

We are acquainted with some of these unique laws in our own world. We see that in the severe, freezing cold of winter when all vegetation is robbed of its verdure and freshness, the pine tree and the box tree withstand the pressure of the murderous cold and preserve their freshness and greenness.

Does the fact that these two trees form an exception to the general condition of plant life mean that the norms and laws governing all plants have been broken? We certainly have no proof establishing in a definite and empirical fashion that the factors and causes we have so far discovered for phenomena are eternally valid, or that nothing can occur in accordance with extraordinary causes.

Numerous scientists tell us today that we must not deny the existence of a whole series of phenomena that do not accord with natural causes, because we do not possess a decisive proof permitting us to negate paranormal phenomena.

Alexis Carrel writes in *The Human Being, the Unknown Being*: "In every country and age, people have believed in the possibility of miraculous and almost immediate cures being effected at shrines and holy places. Today those beliefs have ben weakened, and many physicians believe those cures to be impossible. Nonetheless, given the testimony we have at our disposal, it is necessary to examine the matter and think it over more carefully. The Lourdes Medical Institute has collected many of these testimonies. Our present information concerning the immediate effect of prayer on the curing of diseases rests on the testimony of persons who had suffered from sicknesses such as tuberculosis of the bones, skin cancer and running sores. The nature of the cure does not differ much from one case to the next: first, a feeling of intense pain, then a complete cure. After a few seconds, minutes or—at most—hours, the wounds heal, no trace of the sickness remains, and the patient's appetite returns."

Although this passage does not apply to miracles, it does point to real occurrences that indicate the existence of phenomena the causes for which are unknown to the human being.

Lesson Five
The Answer of the Prophets
to the Illogical Demand of the Polytheists

Without doubt, extreme self-worship, going to extremes in self-worship and in distorting reality and ignoring it, causes the human being's misguidance to increase, together with the dominance of personal, arbitrary inclination over his mind. A true orientation to reality, a decisive entry onto the path of truth, requires the human being to empty his inner being of all obstinate tendencies, the negative consequences of which are irreparable. Everyone has the individual duty of seeking the truth, and this can be attained only by following the path of salvation.

The Quran recognizes as logical that miracles be demanded of the Prophets as proofs of the veracity of their claim, and it narrates in detail the practical and affirmative answer given by the Prophets to this demand of mankind. Nonetheless, there were certain obstinate and illogical persons in each age who were in effect unwilling to accept the truth and demanded from the Prophets miracles of their own choosing. Sometimes they even demanded the performance of deeds that were rationally impossible. Naturally enough, the Prophets who were in communication with the source of revelation did not submit to their childish and obstinate demands. The purpose of miracles is to bear witness to messengerhood, and this aim is accomplished by any miraculous deed that gives assurance that a Prophet has indeed received a mission from God.

Is it necessary that Prophets should produce miracles corresponding to the particular taste and desire of everyone? Must a Divine miracle be subordinate to the will of frivolous and aimless individuals?

The Prophets proclaimed to the human beings that they were entrusted with the guidance and teaching of mankind, so the occurrence of miracles had to be based on the will and desire of God and the necessities of the situation; it was not a means for entertaining illogical and obstinate people. The Noble Quran says: *"No Messenger had the right to perform a miracle without God's permission."* (40:78)

One of the reasons for the Prophets' refusal to submit to those who were demanding miracles of them may have been that those persons imagined the Prophets to be claiming some kind of control over the whole of the universe. The Quran therefore says: *"Tell people I am a human being like you, except that revelation comes to me."* (41:6) *"Say: God is transcendent and elevated. Am I more than a the human being whom God has chosen as His Messenger?"* (17:92)

However, when people were seeking guidance and pursuing the truth, and the Prophets themselves wished to establish the truth of their mission, miracles took place, as is evident from many such instances in the case of Moses, upon whom be peace.

It is always possible for God to draw the attention of the human beings to a miracle in some spectacular way. For example, He can cause inanimate objects and plants to speak or do other remarkable things in order to establish the veracity of His religion. However, such miracles would not be conducive to the human being's freedom or his conscious choice and development. Therefore, God has not acted in this fashion and He has not sought to guide the human being at the expense of his intellectual freedom.

Those who turn their back on the truth will naturally come to experience the result of their deeds and the consequence of their behavior. It is thus that everything moves forward in this world in complete harmony. If God were to punish all humans immediately because of their misdeeds, no one would be able to endure it, for if every wrongdoer were to be killed, the human race would inevitably come to an end.

If those opposing the Prophets had no aim other than uncovering the truth, they would come to accept it both as a result of their own extensive and comprehensive reflections and of the manifest miracles displayed to them. However, the manner in which they demand miracles indicates an evil intention on their part, and a tendency to make unjustifiable objections, not a real search for the truth.

The basic concern of these obstinate persons whose hearts had died within them was denial and turning away from the truth, for considering the existence of clear miracles there was no need for them to be repeated. Even if they had been repeated, those deniers would still not have believed. The Quran says: *"When the Messenger of Truth was sent to them by Us, they said, 'Why has he not been given what Moses was given?' But did they not disbelieve in what had been given to Moses?"* (28:48)

Many of their demands did not even accord with the conditions of a miracle. Thus, the Quran tells us that they proposed the following to the Prophet of Islam: *"...to prove your mission you must bring God and the angels here to us."* (25:24)

In another verse, their foolish objections and expectations along the same lines are analyzed as follows: *"They said: 'We will not believe in you unless you make a spring gush forth for us from the ground, or have a garden of date trees and vines with water flowing through it, or cause the sky to fall in on our heads, or make God and His angels appear in front of us, or have a house covered with gold, or ascend into the sky. But we will not believe in your ascending into the sky unless you bring for us a book we can read.' Say: 'Glory be unto my Lord! Am I anything more than a human being, sent by God with a mission?'"* (17:90-93)

It is evident from these verses that the objectors were demanding from the Messenger of God that, in order to prove his prophethood and his special relationship with the origin of all existence, he should perform miracles such as causing a spring to gush out of the ground or possessing an orchard overflowing with fruit or a palace of god, these being the marks of aristocratic opulence in that age.

It was possible for those demands to be fulfilled, for certain individuals possessed one or all of the things mentioned; however, they were not Prophets.

The possession of material resources can never be a criterion for prophethood and the ability to perform miracles; such things can never be accepted from anyone as a proof of prophethood. This shows how short-sighted and banal they were in their thinking; they imagined illusory power, wealth, and abundance, to constitute criteria for leadership.

Another demand of these tricksters, who were interested in

nothing more than enjoying the same kind of entertainment that the deeds of an ascetic might have provided, was the immediate descent of Divine punishment, bringing human life to an end. But the ultimate aim of the miracle is something quite different: to guide the human beings and make them aware, to nurture their capacities and to liberate them from attachments. It is for this reason that as a result of his accepting the truth, the human being begins to act within a new system of thought.

As for the demand that God and the angels should descend, considering the fact that God is not a body and is not limited with respect to time and space, He cannot have a material or relative manifestation. To imagine the contrary is the result of childish and illogical thinking.

God's final answer to the illegitimate objections of the miracle-seekers is explicit and clear: *"Say: 'Glory be unto my Lord! Am I anything more than a human being, sent by God with a mission?' "*

Through these words, the Prophet fully absolves God from any weakness or inability, while, at the same time, emphasizing his own utter powerlessness to produce miracles of himself. Miracles proceed from the will of God's unlimited essence and the Prophet follows His will. Without God's permission, he has no right to intervene in the workings of the universe, and under no circumstances can he surrender to every demand made on him for the performance of miracles.

Another objection that was made was that they considered the Prophet's belonging to the same human species as themselves a point of weakness. They imagined that Prophets could not be raised up from within society, from among the masses. This, too, the Prophet answers with the same words, condemning thereby the narrow and erroneous view that was a result of their failure to understand the meaning of a prophetic mission. With the lesson and message contained in these words, he barred the path to any deviant interpretation of prophecy and messengerhood.

Still more amazing was that the polytheists used to say: *"We will not believe until we receive what was given to the other Prophets."* (6:124) For those who have no intention of changing and do not wish to be liberated from bondage to their obstinate illusions in order to enter the straight path of guidance, the repetition of a miracle would be entirely fruitless.

An Inadequate Analysis

Those whose thoughts lack a foundation of religious belief attempt to explain the question of revelation and the teachings of the Prophets as follows: those teachings did not have a heavenly origin, but arose instead from the intellectual genius of those pure and outstanding humanitarians. Since the peoples that lived in the time of the Prophets could not be convinced by the logic of reason, in order to gain their support, the Prophets attributed to God the laws and regulations they themselves had drawn up which were indeed useful for the reform of corrupt societies.

This interpretation of the matter is neither logical nor realistic, for however much abundant talent and innate genius an individual possesses, his talents will remain buried and his genius unfulfilled unless he receives instruction and education. By contrast, the knowledge of the Prophets was not learned or acquired; they did not acquire learning from some masters with whom they were contemporary. In addition, the work of geniuses unfolds in accordance with material and natural principles, whereas the miracles of the Prophets are not based on natural and conventional laws or formulae.

If they had no source other than genius and perspicacious intelligence, unless they had discovered some entirely new factor, the teachings they promulgated after claiming prophethood would have to have had some antecedent, and they would have developed their thoughts and ideas gradually, not suddenly and all at once.

By contrast, all the profound transformations we see in the lives of the Prophets begin, without exception, at the moment they proclaim themselves to be Prophets. Before that moment, putting aside their abundant spirituality and inward purity, everything in the external circumstances of the Prophets is entirely normal.

This abrupt transformation, this sudden presentation of teachings that within a comprehensive theoretical and practical framework orient the thoughts and actions of the human being toward a specific goal—his liberation from domination by natural and social forces—is clear evidence and proof that a new factor has entered the lives of the Prophets, that a new gushing source for the discovery of truth has been placed at their disposal.

Nowhere in the course of human history will we encounter persons the products of whose talent and the fruit of whose genius make such a sudden, abrupt appearance. However, this was precisely the case with the Prophets.

Any impartial researcher who examines the history of the Prophets will realize that the entirety of their noble lives was characterized by truthfulness, honesty, devotion to the truth, and love of humanity. Particularly apparent in their lives were their spirit of self-sacrifice, their endurance of pressure and overwhelming problems, and their constructive determination at all times to advance toward fulfilling their goal. Even their hate-filled enemies were obliged to credit them with all these virtues.

These qualities demonstrate well what constituted the foundation on which the Prophets stood in their mission devoted to truth and humanity, while confronting the inhumane and impure elements that always emerged to confront the men of God.

Given this, can we attribute the utterance of falsehood, for the sake of gaining greater influence in society, to persons who represent an ideal model of freedom from all crookedness and deviousness? Is it permissible to accuse of making false and unfounded statements personages in whose conduct we see not the slightest trace of selfish desire?

It was precisely their lofty and worthy conduct that accelerated their success in winning over a whole segment of mankind that was drowning in the stagnant waters of ignorance. Furthermore, one of the principal teachings put forward by those men of God, one of the hallmarks of their mission, was a summons to honesty and truthfulness and a condemnation of hypocrisy and deviousness.

Specimens of Human Perfection According to Ali, upon whom be peace

In one of his speeches, Ali, upon whom be peace, discusses the lives of the Prophets, describing those most exalted exemplars of human virtue as follows: "Let me speak of the characteristics of Moses, to whom God spoke. When he raised his hands in prayer to the presence of his Lord, he swore and affirmed, 'O God, I need nothing of all Your bounty save only a piece of bread to relieve my hunger.' He asked for nothing more because in his indigence he used to ward off hunger with the wild grasses of the desert, and so this was he that the greenness of the grass he used to consume was visible through the diaphanous skin of his stomach.

"Let me mention David, the Prophet who first introduced reed pipes. He would weave baskets from date fibre, and then ask his companions, 'Which of you will buy this basket?' He would buy barley bread with the money he earned from selling the baskets and eat it.

"Let me speak of Jesus, son of Mary, upon whom be peace. He would place a stone beneath his head to sleep on at night; he always wore coarse clothing and passed his days in hunger. The moon was his lamp in the darkness of the night, and the azure roof of the heavens was his shelter in winter. He prepared his food from the plants that grew in the ground; he had neither a spouse to draw his attention to her nor a child on whom to lavish anxious care. He had no wealth calling for his attention, nor greed and desire to abase him with the search for riches. His only mount was his own two feet, and his two hands were always at work in the service of God's creatures.

"Follow your own Prophet of pure disposition, Muhammad, upon whom be peace and blessings. He was a perfect example of all human virtues. God loves those who in the conduct of their lives follow His Messenger, who place their feet in his footsteps, and who follow him in their choice of a way of life. He took but a slight portion of the life of this world.

"His nurture was dry bread, and he never ate to satiation. They offered him the world, and he did not accept it. He disliked whatever God disliked, and he despised whatever God regarded as lowly.

"When he ate, he would sit on the ground. He would sit and stand with the meekness of a slave. He would mend his own clothes and stitch his own shoes. A simple curtain covered the door to his dwelling, and he would tell his wives to remove it, because it reminded him of the worldly life and its adornments.

"Even within his heart, he would wage war against worship of the world, obliterating all consciousness of it from his heart. He expelled all concern for worldly well-being from his mind and closed his eyes to all adornment and luxury.

"Every possessor of intelligence must ask himself whether God was honoring the Prophet through this way of life or, on the contrary, humiliating and abasing him. If he says that God was abasing him, he has spoken in error and accused God of a monstrosity.

"So follow the Prophet in the conduct of your lives, for it is he who holds the banner of resurrection and who provides the measure by which all humans deeds are to be measured. He entered the arena of this world with a pure intelligence and conscience and passed through this world, closing his eyes to the things of the world for the sake of God's message. He never placed one stone on top of another in order to build himself a dwelling, and he never constructed a palace.

"How grateful we should be to God that in His kindness and favor sent us Muhammad, upon whom be peace, for us to follow and take as our model, and to follow step by step the path he traced out with his life."[8]

The way of recognizing Prophets is not restricted to the miracles they performed. Indeed, the method prescribed by reason and knowledge represents the most profound way of recognizing a Prophet, particularly in an age when the intellect has developed and knowledge has advanced. Through careful examination and objective analysis, by taking into consideration both individual and social characteristics, as well as the content of the teachings being proclaimed, it is possible to recognize the true Prophet, and to do so, in fact, at a more profound level than do those who merely witness the miracles they perform.

A distinct school of thought can present itself to researchers and investigators more effectively and convincingly than by means of a miracle; it can demonstrate the veracity of the program it proposes.

The clearest, most evidential and primary proof of a correct school of thought, in an age when knowledge and learning are fully present, is its complete conformity with the criteria of science and the observable realities of the universe. It should, therefore, be realized that if a school of thought does not accord with the criteria of science, and if, from the point of view of its content and regulations, it contradicts science and free thought, that school definitely has no relation to the Creator.

It is thus that with the advancement of knowledge and the intellectual development of society, the authentic teachings of the

Prophets—which ensure the perfection of the human being, provide for his spiritual and material needs, and enable both the individual and society to grow and advance, shine ever more strongly through the darkness of illusion and superstition and display their brilliant visage ever more clearly. The heavenly nature of the Prophets, which is clearly delineated in the Quran, is an indication of their lofty standing and status before the Creator.

A whole separate *surah* was revealed concerning the Prophet Noah. He has such an exalted status that God invokes peace on him in the following terms: *"Peace be upon Noah and greetings be unto him! Thus do we reward the doers of good, for he was truly one of our believing servants."* (37:79-80)   The Quran mentions Abraham, upon whom be peace, the champion of Divine unity, as follows: *"God chose Abraham as His friend."* (4:125) *"It is fitting for the believers that they should follow Abraham."* (60:4) *"He was a grateful servant of his Lord."* (17:) *"He was a truthful bestower of counsel."* (11:107)

Concerning Solomon, that just ruler, He says: *"We bestowed Solomon on David; he was a virtuous servant who turned always to God."* (38:30)

God granted him His favor and generosity in both worlds, as is apparent from these two verses: *"This is a limitless bounty bestowed in this world."* (38:39) *"For Solomon there shall be a goodly return in the next world, and a station of nearness in the presence of his Lord."* (38:40)

Concerning David, God says: *"Mention Our servant David. He was most powerful, and he constantly turned to Our presence in repentance. We strengthened his kingdom and rule, and gave him the power to perceive truths and to distinguish the true from the false."* (38:17-18)

God mentions Joseph, that veracious one who taught all seekers of virtue the lesson of struggle against sin, in the following terms: *"Joseph who had heard these words, raised up his hands in supplication and said: 'O God, the torment of prison is more preferable to me than the ugly deed the women demand of me.'"* (12:33)

Finally, expressing the respect that is due all of the Prophets, He says: *"God's peace and blessings be upon His cherished Messengers."* (37:181)

Lesson Six
What is revelation?

Within the overall scheme of being, revelation is the precise, complex and unique relationship that links the Prophets to God. It is the sole source for the knowledge of prophethood, the basis for the cognition and insights of the Prophets, and the vehicle for their exalted mission of bringing about fundamental and positive change in human society. Through their superior, clear and direct awareness of the realities of being, the Prophets are inspired by God with heavenly teachings and laws, which they then present to the human beings as messages from the realm of the unseen.

The process of revelation consists of an angel softly conveying certain matters to the hearing of a Prophet. Sometimes the Prophet sees the angel and exchanges words with him. If matters are conveyed only to the heart, this is a question of inspiration, not of revelation.

Prophets who shone forth in the darkness at a time when discrimination, injustice and disunion had reached their height, began their missions with a command received through revelation. By arousing human beings' minds, they directed their attention to the subtle perceptions latent within their own primordial nature and attempted to cleanse them of the effects left by the beliefs and customs they had acquired from their environment. Thus they were able to make blossom the higher capacities and urges of the human being and to guide them towards happiness and the good.

Of course, the ultimate nature of revelation and the type of perception that leads to it is not known to us, because it lies beyond the categories accessible to normal perception and the forms of awareness that are available to the human being through the operation of his creative intellect on the data and knowledge that he acquires. Despite the spiritual and intellectual legacies that have been passed down to us, we are unable to perceive the particular characteristics of this relationship with God. This has always remained a dark corner inaccessible to our thought and imagination, and it may always remain so.

Nonetheless, it is certain that abundant spirituality and extraordinary inward purity in a given individual may create in him a certain receptivity that fits him to receive God's abundant revelation and to be chosen for undertaking the mission of a Prophet.

At the same time, being actually able to receive heavenly commands and to be linked to the pre-eternal source of revelation depends exclusively on the will of God. The purity and worthiness of an individual cannot be a causative factor in the establishment of that relationship.

Since the purpose of prophethood is the comprehensive guidance of the individual and society toward perfection and the laying down of a legal system and a social order for mankind, the assumption of responsibility involved is necessarily heavy and taxing. To accept bearing the burden of prophethood requires great capacity and energy. God therefore bestows the station of prophethood on those who have the ability and capacity to bear the heavy responsibilities of delineating a practical course for the human being to follow through the light of revelation.

Being appointed to this mission is like a storm that envelops the whole being of the Prophet. It causes his mind to overflow with the light of insight and wisdom, and by virtue of this clarity of vision, as well as his freedom from arbitrary and selfish desires and erroneous thought, he mobilizes all his capacities with an inexhaustible ardor to fulfil his Divine mission.

Iqbal, the celebrated thinker of the Indian subcontinent, compares the Prophets with other spiritual personalities whom he calls mystics. Although what he has to say is interesting, the comparison of Prophets with mystics is inadequate.

"The mystic does not wish to return from the repose of 'unitary experience'; and even when he does return, as he must, his return does not mean much for mankind at large. The Prophet's return is creative. He returns to insert himself into the sweep of time with a view to control the forces of history, and thereby to create a fresh world of ideals. For the mystic, the repose of 'unitary experience' is something final; for the Prophet it is the awakening, within him, of world-shaking psychological forces, calculated to completely transform the human world."[9]

The phenomenon of revelation neither contradicts the norms of creation nor is it possible to find in philosophy or those of the natural sciences that have not been contaminated by dogmatic prejudices masquerading as science, any proof for the impossibility of such a relationship between the human being and God, for the content of revelation does not constitute a category opposed to science. It is possible that in the course of time science will advance to a point where it can show interesting findings in this area.

As we know, being is infinite; therefore, the possibility of knowledge and perception also extends toward the infinite. In our judgment of matters we should not imagine that we are able, within our own limited historical period, to comprehend the entirety of being and its complex realities in their majesty and infinitude. Rather we must hope that as human knowledge expands and increases, certain mysteries will be disclosed to us and matters of which we are now ignorant will become clarified.

The ability of the Prophets to communicate with God, to receive and pass on messages from the world of the unseen without any material instruments, is in no way inferior to a radio receiver and transmitter; on the contrary, its effectiveness is much greater and stronger than that of any instrument manufactured by humans.

At night, ships on the ocean make use of radar in order to find out about other ships approaching, and radar can also be used to send pilotless planes to whatever destination may be desired. If the human mind can produce radar waves, why cannot it not also emit and receive other waves that are unknown to us and unrecognized by us? Is the human being less than the instrument he has created himself?

Once we understand the truths suggested by these questions, we can no longer assume an attitude of denial when faced with mysterious and complex phenomena. With a profound understanding of phenomena, and with a wide panorama open in front of him, human being's consciousness and culture will ultimately reach a point where many truths and mysteries will be unfolded before him.

Although the human being has sense perception in common with the animals, some senses are far more highly developed in certain animals than in the human being. There are mysterious forms of perception in animals that scientists are unable to comprehend.

It is not necessary that waves should be transmitted by means of metal instruments. Moths have something similar to radar waves, so, in principle, we may say that waves can be produced, received and emitted by flesh, skin and bones. Would it be correct to regard the human being as less than a moth?

An animal can be blindfolded and transported hundreds of kilometers away from its home, but astonishingly it is able to make its way back. What capacity and what type of perception is it that enables it to return to its original location? What capacity is it that gives rise to this remarkable, unerring sense of direction? What instrument produces these rays, and in accordance with what frequency?

Scientists have undertaken different experiments to understand how birds find their direction, but they have never been able to neutralize this capacity either in a bird or in any other animal.

Numerous waves are broadcast from every corner of the globe, waves which may be received elsewhere, yet we are totally unaware of them. We do not yet understand the true nature of energy, of light, or of waves, so how can we grant ourselves the right to deny revelation which arises from the elevated nature, the pure vision, and the special relationship of Divinely chosen personages with God? Does the fact that such a relationship is unavailable to us constitute a proof of its impossibility for everyone?

There is no scientific proof negating the possibility of revelation. The fact that science has been unable, down to the present, to discern the sources of revelation does not mean that the fact of revelation should be regarded as a scientifically unacceptable phenomenon.

When we cannot fully solve, with some scientific interpretation, the problem of the unique and astonishing perceptions and sense that are used by animals to guide them in their existence; when we cannot comprehend the nature of the mysterious transmitter that is secreted in certain birds, enabling them to communicate with the opposite sex over great distances—given these inabilities, how can we insist on trying with the methods of the empirical sciences to solve the problem of revelation, the unique relationship existing between one exalted human being and the source of all being?

If the phenomenon of revelation lies outside the scope of sense perception and experimentation, and human knowledge has been unable, up to the present, to clarify this kind of reality, why should the impotence of science in this area arouse doubt and hesitation in us? The French scholar de la Mane says concerning the impossibility of knowing the ultimate reality and essence of God: "What a fool is the denier who says, 'since I do not understand His true essence, therefore, He does not exist.!' If he can define a single grain of sand, I will bring God before him!"

Revelation is a particular mode of awareness and perception that occurs in certain rare individuals. The nature of that awareness is clear enough to them, and if it is unknowable to others, it is because they do not find in themselves that mysterious super-awareness. However, through studying the properties and effects of that form of awareness, they can discern the truth or falsehood of those who lay claim to it and see whether or not they truly possess that great and abundant source of knowledge.

Revelation in the Quran

The word revelation is used frequently in the Noble Quran, and its various occurrences demonstrate that revelation is not confined to human beings. However, the unfolding of revelation is connected to the general progress of all beings toward perfection, and the highest stage of revelation, which the human being alone is fitted to receive from the world of the unseen, consists of that which God sends to His chosen Messengers based on the need of them for Divine guidance.

All phenomena—whether it be the plants that raise their heads above the soil, in the planets, the constellations, and the sun which aid us with their heat, their light and their rotation—benefit the human being by fulfilling their functions in accordance with a certain type of revelation.

The laws and the order which govern the whole expanse of being and on the basis of which all things take shape, demonstrate that the whole of being is imprinted with a certain revealed law.

The entire universe is, then, never deprived, even for an instant, of the favor of God's law.

Once we see matters in this light, is there any phenomenon which can be said to lie beyond the scope of God's revelation? Is not obedience to the order of creation a form of worship, one which involves neither logic nor knowledge? God provides for the needs of the infant even before its birth by placing milk, the most appropriate form of sustenance for it, in the reservoir of the mother's breast, so that the sustenance of the child is ready for it as soon as it enters the world. Why then should it not be possible for God as Sustainer to have prepared in advance the life-giving food needed by human beings and societies as they evolve, thereby providing future generations with the appropriate and necessary sustenance?

Considering the fact that revelation is not restricted to the human being, and the will of God and His signs are at work in the ordering of the sun and the moon and the succession of day and night, the revelation sent to the Prophets may also be said to lie at the very heart of the mechanism of the universe, following its general and comprehensive laws while preserving its own distinctive features. This should not be taken to negate the role of the human being as a free and independent being living within the world of contingencies; the assistance rendered unilaterally by nature to the human being does not diminish his value and standing.

Clearly, the spirit of every individual human being does not receive revelation; not everyone can establish a direct relationship with the heavenly realm and receive laws and ordinances from God without intermediary. One of the reasons for this is that humans as a species are strongly subject to instinctual desires and material causes and limitations; this constitutes an obstacle which prevents the human being from attaining the conditions necessary for a direct relationship with the supramaterial realm. In addition, as was pointed out above, the receipt of commands from heaven depends entirely on God's will. Thus the Quran says: "*God knows best where to place His message.*" (6:122)

Without recourse to some instrument, we cannot hear the waves that are broadcast by transmitters throughout the world, so we need an instrument with two complementary capacities: on the one hand, it must receive the waves in the air exactly as they are transmitted, and, on the other, it must convey them to our ear. Failing this, we will be unable to benefit from the waves that are being broadcast.

Likewise, mankind similarly needs those outstanding individuals who have two complementary properties: on the one hand, they will be linked to the material dimensions of human life, and, on the other hand, on account of certain powerful spiritual capacities, they will be in simultaneous contact with two worlds. Those individuals are, of course, the Prophets, who on account of possessing these two properties have been chosen by the Creator as highly evolved beings able to receive His message. Having received from the source of all being those positive, constructive commands of God and the elevated principles of culture that derive from them, they then convey them to the inhabitants of the world.

Lesson Seven
The Difference Between Prophets and Scholars of Genius

The Steadfastness of the Prophets in Conveying their Message

Who can deny the distinctive sincerity of the Prophets, the profound faith that is anchored in the depths of their beings, and the creative exertions they make in order to convey their teachings and message? Who can belittle their uncompromising struggle against corruption and oppression? If we deny the sincerity and pure intention of the Prophets, the progress made by their teachings and the ability of their message to conquer the hearts and spirits of nations cannot be possibly be explained.

One, the unique decisiveness shown by the Prophets in propagating their message and defending their message, their sense of urgent necessity, points to that message being something quite different from the scientific theories put forth by scholars. Whenever scientific personalities wish to put forward their views, they cannot disregard the possibility of those views being invalidated, however firmly they may be based on the most advanced scientific knowledge. Since immobility is unacceptable on the path to the future advancement of knowledge, they do not block the path to additional and scientifically more acceptable research. Continuous and unceasing effort may result in the supplementing or modification of their views.

This was not the method of the Prophets. They believed profoundly in what they said, and in carrying out and advancing the mission contained in revelation, they unhesitatingly refused to retreat even a single step. They pursued their call strenuously and with steadfastness, and went forward even at the risk of their lives with their campaigns to bring about change and convey to human beings those Divine principles of culture that inspire the human being to ascend.

Two, to rely on devious methods, to have recourse to trickéry, deceit and lies, creates anxiety; to act contrary to the truth arouses disquiet and unease. History does not provide a single example of a bearer of Divine revelation who manifested the least sign of anxiety.

This striking characteristic of the Prophets permits us to grasp the profound reason why they conveyed their message, and gave to mankind the glad tidings of salvation through following their teachings, clearly, directly, with the utmost confidence, and without any preliminary.

The task of the Prophets was utterly removed from any kind of trickery or deceit; their teachings were profoundly rooted in the realities of being and linked to the true source of all knowledge and awareness.

Three, furthermore, scholars frequently fall prey to error in their views. A given researcher can often be seen to express contradictory views on the same subject in the course of his career, and it is impossible to find a single scholar who has not made a single mistake in the course of his life.

Einstein says: "Not many scholars can be found today who regard themselves as qualified to put forward something as a definitive truth. On the contrary, figures such as Newton admit that what appears today to them today to be clear may be regarded by future generations as confused and obscure. Our descendents may look at our works of our predecessors."[10]

By contrast, the scheme of creation is not subject to error in the guidance it dispenses to the human being on obtaining his material needs. Similarly, in guiding the human being to his ultimate goal, it provides him with unerring revelation that derives from the same source as the laws of creation and points together with them to the same goal.

There is no instance in the history of prophethood of a Prophet taking back what he had previously said, after once enunciating the Divine message, or of his admitting an error and negating his previous program in order to substitute new teachings. By contrast, the ideas of thinkers are frequently seen to change as the horizons of scientific thought expand. The abrogation of a certain revealed ordinance does not contradict what we have said concerning the Prophets. First, a temporary ordinance is revealed in order to assure a certain limited benefit, and later it loses its validity with the issuance of a second, more comprehensive ordinance.

Four, the successes attained by scientists and scholars in discovering certain truths come gradually and pre-suppose the completion of courses of study and experimentation. Much time passes between the first stage of his work, when he begins his efforts to uncover something, and its final stages.

But when we look at the lives of the Prophets, we see that they had no need of any preliminaries in order to uncover the truth, nor were they subject to any hesitation. Instead, the truths they received came to them in all their dimensions directly from the source of being, without their passing through various stages of learning and investigation, and they proclaimed those truths immediately.

Five, if we look at the fundamental emphases in the teachings of the Prophets, at the great variety and comprehensiveness that is to be seen in every aspect of them, in a precise and analytical fashion, not in a purely abstract, superficial and limited framework, we will come to appreciate more profoundly how those teachings constitute a complete school of thought, liberating the human being in every sense of the word.

Again, if we examine the firm foundations and principles on which religions are based, we will realize that none of their principal elements correspond to the views and utterances of the scholars that lived in those times. Considering the unfavorable conditions of the environment, the intellectual decay of the societies in which the Prophets were raised, it is impossible that the fruitful and elevated principles contained in every Divine message should have derived from the thoughts of a man.

Never in human history, in the course of the overall development of human society, have thinkers and men of learning been seen to produce such texts that overflow with spirituality and awareness, that in their comprehensiveness relate to all the concerns and stages of individual and social life, and that have had such a profound and observable effect. The teachings of the Prophets have had special characteristics, representing the richest and most vital source of culture in the ages when they made their appearance.

Six, choosing to accept the path of the Prophets is not simply an abstract or creedal matter that remains exclusively in the sphere of belief. Through accepting that path, human beings are, in reality, choosing a method fo life, a special mode of existence, that leaves its imprint on their outer conduct. The Divine worldview is not merely an intellectual infrastructure for it also has distinctive superstructures that in their aggregate give shape to human behavior and the fabric of society.

It is possible to attribute such abundant sources of life, such comprehensive teachings that lead to the growth and improvement of the human being, to any source other than Divine revelation? For the teachings of the Prophets all exude the scent of authentic Divine message.

The investigations of researchers make it plain that the efforts of scientists and scholars take place in isolation from each other. Each travels his own path in seeking solutions to scientific problems, and they are unconcerned with the efforts of others as they pursue their researches. If their theories occasionally become interconnected in the course of their investigations, this is because of the interrelatedness of scientific questions with each other, without this being intended by the researchers in question.

Matters are quite different in the case of the Prophets. Not only do they consider the books received by their predecessors to be valid, they also confirm their missions and praise their efforts and strivings. This proves that all heavenly religions have but one source of inspiration, with each serving to supplement and perfect is predecessor.

If we look carefully at the preaching of the Prophets, we see that each of them was required to confirm those who had preceded him, and it may also have been necessary that each should proclaim the mission of the next Prophet to follow him. The abrogation of a religion does not mean its invalidation; its consists rather in the proclamation of a new and more complete message. God-given knowledge cannot be invalidated; it is simply that the following Prophet states it more fully and more precisely. The same applies to changes in divine ordinances.

Addressing the Prophet of Islam, the Glorious Quran says: *"In truth We have sent the Quran to you, confirming all the previous heavenly books that were revealed before you and bearing witness to them."* (5:48) *"When God took the covenant of the Prophets, saying, 'I give you a book and wisdom,' then there came to guide you, O People of the Book, a messenger from God who bore witness to the truth of your book and your law so that you might believe in him and aid him. God said, 'Do you accept My messenger and that which I have sent in his heavenly book, the Quran?' They all said, 'We accept.' God said, 'Be witnesses over yourselves and your peoples, and I too will be a witness with you over them."* (3:81)

The Bible similarly relates these words from Jesus, upon whom be peace: "Do not think that I have come to invalidate the Torah or the scrolls of the Prophets. I have come not to invalidate, but to fulfil."[11]

The truths enunciated in these quotations are an eloquent proof of the unity linking together the missions of all of the Prophets. Their teachings took wing in the direction of infinity, having no source other than the all-penetrating will of God, the revelation of the Creator. Since the clear and conscious faith of the Prophets was profoundly linked to the origin of all being, decisiveness, self-reliance and steadfastness came to be their special characteristics.

Lesson Eight
The Inerrancy of the Prophets

Taking on the grave and sensitive responsibilities of prophethood and the guidance of society requires the possession of a whole series of exalted and previous qualities, without which a person will never be fit to assume a position of leadership.

One of the exceptional qualities required in a Prophet is that there should exist within him a restraining force that, arising from the perfection of his faith and the intensity of his piety, protects him against not only the commission of sins and acts of moral corruption but also from considering them or intending to commit them, so that throughout the entirety of his life, both before and after the beginning of his mission, all dimensions of his being should be free of the dark blemish of sin.

There can be no doubt that the more crucial the position of an individual in society, the deeper is his need for public trust and confidence. Now can any position be graver and carry more responsibility than that of the Prophet who is to guide society, exercising his guidance in all affairs of life, both spiritual and material?

The supreme purpose and aim of the mission of God's Messengers is to guide and educate human beings across the world by means of a series of Divine teachings and ordinances. It is, at the same time, the religious duty of mankind to submit to all the sublime injunctions of religion that the Prophet has presented as revelation and Divine law. Naturally, humans will implement those teachings with all their heart and soul and accord absolute value to them only when they are thoroughly convinced that those teachings do indeed emanate from the source of all being.

What authority or person can earn such universal trust that whatever he says will earn sincere and unquestioning acceptance so that human beings submit to his commands? Can anyone deserve that trust unless he is armed with the weapon of inerrancy and virtue is manifest in him in all its dimensions?

Were it not possible to trust completely a Messenger of God in his receiving and conveying the revelation, the aim of prophethood—which is the perfection of humanity—could not be ensured; were the Prophets to lack inerrancy in conveying the Commands of God, society would inevitably deviate from its true course.

Were the Prophets not to be protected from pollution by sin and infection by moral disease, and were they not to gain immunity from all kinds of impurity, the possibility would always exist that they would stumble when confronted with the deceptive allure of the material world and pursue personal goals such as wealth and power. This would be true even if they had lofty human attributes to a superior degree. It is obvious that the existence of such a possibility would cause their followers to hesitate before implementing the commands and pronouncements.

The one who claims prophethood and the right to lead human beings, whom human beings must follow in order to attain the pinnacle of perfection in all aspects of their life—if such a one were to have the slightest record of deviance, dishonesty and inclination to sin, could it be totally excluded that he would never again life, betray or speak an untruth? Could he be accepted as a model of virtue and purity?

Without doubt, intelligence and logic compel us to answer this question in the negative. No one could accept with complete confidence as revelation and the Command of God the words of someone whose life did not shine with purity, who had fallen into the whirlpool of sin and openly engaged in corruption and moral turpitude before claiming prophethood, even though later a spiritual revolution and transformation had occurred in him. No one could accept his teachings as an unquestionable message from heaven, particularly with regard to matters that lie beyond the experience of the human being.

The Prophets must also be completely removed from anything that causes doubt to arise or impairs the completeness of God's proof. The Quran proclaims: *"Before this, you were unable to read or to write; this was lest the deniers should doubt concerning your pro-*

phethood." (29:47) *"Say: God's is the best and most eloquent proof. "* (10:47) *"We sent the Prophets as givers of glad tidings and warnings so that no excuse should remain thereafter for human beings."* (4:165)

Therefore the first necessary condition for the appearance of revelation is the absolute sincerity and inner purity of the Prophets. The burning love of human beings for the Prophets and their devotion to them which arises from the deepest layers of their inner being as well as their belief in absolute values, in God, and the guardians of religion—all of this is made possible by the inerrancy and perfection of those Divinely guided personages.

The effectiveness of conduct and mode of action is infinitely greater than that of mere words. The behavior and attributes of a teacher plays a fundamental role in the instruction of those for whom he is responsible, action having a far-reaching effect in building the character of an individual that cannot in any way be compared with the effect of speech.

It will be a disaster for humanity if the one who assumes a lofty position of spiritual guidance in society is himself immersed in a whirlpool of pollution and evil. If he lacks true awareness and piety, can he create an appropriate environment for the fostering of virtue, and can he bring about an inward transformation and revolution in the human being that will have a lasting effect? Will he have the capacity to train human beings and be their moral guide? Can he implant piety and virtue in their minds and their thoughts?

The commission of even a single sin by the Prophets would render fruitless their attempts at nurturing human beings to attain perfection, which is the goal of their mission. How can one who is himself polluted with sin purify others of their sins? One who is not himself morally and spiritually perfect cannot possibly succeed in training human beings to perfection.

We cannot take into consideration only the deeds and conduct of the Prophets during the period of their mission, and treat them separately from the spiritual and ethical characteristics they display during the rest of their lives. A more comprehensive investigation must be carried, for it is not enough that Prophets turn to purity only at the beginning of their missions.

The firm and continuous link of the Prophets with the source of existence and the complete absence of pollution by sin throughout all of their lives constitute an absolute necessity. Divinely guided personalities must never have been polluted by sin. Any prior record of sin on their part will form a great obstacle in the path of their heavenly mission which is to guide human beings to God and call them to purity and the avoidance of all abomination.

One who until yesterday stood in the ranks of the impure, those polluted by corruption, and who devoted a whole segment of his life to sin, will inevitably have his evil record remembered by others; it will be vividly present in their minds, and they cannot overlook it as they analyze and sit in judgment on his past life. The beginning of a profound spiritual transformation cannot by itself wash away all previous corruption and remove it from the minds of human beings.

When studying the histories of the Prophets, one should never content oneself with a superficial listing of events. The perceptive researcher must investigate all the different dimensions of the lives of the Prophets before their assumption of the prophethood. Then only will they be able to understand why the obstinate sworn enemies of the Prophets, in their conspiratorial efforts to prevent the dissemination of the heavenly message, do not shrink even from attributing madness to the Prophets, but never dare to accuse them of moral corruption.

The character and personality of the Prophets were so well-known and so brilliant to their contemporaries that such an idiotic accusation on the part of their enemies would have caused people to reject their other accusations as well and thus nullified all their long-standing efforts.

If the Prophets had been sullied by even as much as a single sin, this would have been used as an effective weapon to destroy their social standing and prestige. It is obvious that point out weaknesses in the past lives of the Prophets and recalling their previous errors and sins would have been a most effective weapon for destroying the repute of the Prophets and shaking people's trust and belief in them. This in itself constitutes vital and eloquent proof that they had already acquired a certain sanctity which characterized both their way of viewing things and their actions.

In the story of Moses we read that Pharaoh, the oppressive tyrant, immediately reminded Moses of his past when he was confronted by him. He addressed him critically as follows: *"'Are*

*you not that child whom we reared and who spent years of his life in our
presence? Did you not kill a man and did you not deny our Divinity?'
Moses answered: 'I did indeed commit that act, but not intentionally. I
was acting only with the intent of saving one who had been wronged, and
the result was an accidental killing. Then I fled because of my fear of you
until God taught me knowledge and wisdom and made me one of the
Prophets.'* " (26.18-21)

Let us recall that the environment in which the Prophets were
raised was encircled by all kinds of darkness and corruption. It was
not an environment in which purity, innocence, and piety might
flourish, or the inner nature of the human being, with its predispo-
sition to the truth, might be nurtured. Such an unfavorable
environment ought surely to have caused the Prophets also to
become polluted by conforming to the social conditions that surrounded them.

However, we see that true awareness, virtue and honor came
into being in precisely the most corrupt of environments, shinning
like so many jewels over the heads of human beings. This in itself
is clear testimony to the different dimensions and aspects of the
personality of the Prophets, the nature of their inerrancy and their
complete moral immunity.

It can also be clearly deduced from the Quran that attaining the
lofty station of prophethood (as well as that of imamate) is possible
only through being free of all contamination by sin and spiritual
evil.

When Abraham addresses the Divine Presence with the peti-
tion that He appoint his descendants as leaders and guides, God
responds by making the avoidance of oppression an explicit condition of prophethood: *"My covenant and the station of prophethood
are given only to those who have not committed any oppression (whether
toward themselves or others)."* (2:123) *"He knows the unseen dimensions
of this world, whereas none knows His world of the unseen except those He
has chosen from among the Prophets, to protect whom He sends angels
from in front and behind. Thus He may know that the Messengers have
fully conveyed the messages of their Creator to mankind.,"* (72:26-28)

So from the point of view of the Quran, which describes the
Prophets by the use of various attributes, it is an essential condition
of prophethood that the Prophet possess inerrancy and never have
been polluted by any act of oppression, for this counts as an

encroachment on God's sanctity. God does not permit the reins of guidance for humanity to fall into the incompetent hands of one whose heart is blackened by sin and whose hands are stained by cruelty and oppression.

The question of the apparent attribution of sins to the Prophets by the Quran can be understood when we examine the type of sins at issue, for there are differences of degree among sins. Veritable and absolute sin lies in rebelling against the commandments of God; the commission of this sin brings punishment and retribution, and God's Messengers are absolutely protected against it.

Another kind of sin is relative; if a human being commits a sin of this category, Divine Law does not provide for punishment or retribution. However, acts of this type would detract from the loftiness of the Prophets and would be totally irreconcilable with their vision and moral refinement.

In social and religious matters, the expectations that are had of different personages are not uniform. The level of expectations depends on the capacities of individuals, together with the position they hold, the knowledge they have, and other matters. If an illiterate person delivers an eloquent and powerful speech, it will be a matter for congratulation, even though the content of the speech, deriving from the thoughts of an undeveloped mind, may be insignificant. But if a serious scholar, whose words ought to create a storm and to leave an impress on the mind, delivers the same kind of speech, it will be regarded as deficient and open to objection.

Let us now draw an analogy with the sublime and majestic personalities of the Prophets. They have vast resources of knowledge and faith, as well as direct access to reality and the richest and most abundant source of awareness and knowledge. Considering this, if for an instant they are neglectful of God—something which would not earn a reproach for others—it will count as a manifest error on their part. The brilliant visage of their prophethood will be clouded and sin will be ascribed to them, for that instant of neglect was not compatible with their lofty personality.

In addition, the position of prophethood and the guidance of mankind is of such crucial importance that if the Prophet commits any error, the honor of the community he leads will also be affected; society will also carry the stain of his shame.

Inerrancy Does Not Negate Free Will

Here the following question arises. If inerrancy is a gift from God, resulting in the protection of the Prophets when faced with abomination and sin, their abstention from sin cannot be conscious and deliberate, nor be regarded as a proof of their superior status or a source of pride for them. For their mental constitution is such that God has guaranteed them immunity from sin.

This objection would be justified if inerrancy were the result of pre-determination, with the commission of any kind of sin being impossible for the Prophets, and the Prophets being compelled to obey God's Commands and acquire virtues and purity of soul. But this is not the case; the inerrancy under discussion is founded on perfect faith and awareness. It demonstrates itself clearly in action, and in no way negates free will and choice.

All the deeds of the leaders of religion, like those of other human beings, arise from free will and consciousness. Why should it be necessary for an external coercive force to push them in the direction of inerrancy? Will any difficulty remain if their vision of the world is seen to play this role? With their profound vision, the Prophets perceive the majesty and splendor of the Supreme and Absolute Power, manifest across the limitless plain of existence, at so sublime a level that their heart and their mind overflow with the love of God. How could it be believed that such highly conscious and excellent beings should stain their hearts with sin and disobey the commandments of their God and Beloved? Furthermore, they are profoundly aware of the awesome consequences of sin, given which it would be impossible for them even to consider committing sins and evil acts.

It is true that knowledge of the evil consequences of sin does not in itself provide immunity against it. However, the inerrancy of the Messengers of God arises from so powerful and realistic a form of knowledge that they are able clearly to see with the eye of their heart the requital that sin brings. It is this that makes it quite impossible for them to commit any sin.

A doctor will never drink from a vessel that is contaminated by a microbe because he knows the dangerous consequences this would entail. Mountaineers spend a whole life climbing mountains, but their intelligence and awareness never allow them even to conceive of the possibility of deliberately falling vertically, let alone undertaking such an act.

Do the doctor and the mountaineer in these two examples have some kind of built-in and involuntary immunity against these irrational acts? Do they avoid these fatal acts without exercising free choice? To drink from the contaminated vessel or not to drink, to fall or not to fall—both alternatives are possible for them, but their conceptualizing of the results and consequences of the fatal acts reduce to near zero the likelihood of their undertaking them.

Here we can grasp clearly the link between knowledge, which is the very kernel of awareness, and action, which is the external manifestation of awareness. We can see how profound and exact mental awareness objectifies itself, and how the human being is situated between cause and effect, between subjective and objective action and reaction.

Similarly, inerrancy in the Prophets proceeds from their profound awareness of the effects of sin, of Divine anger and punishment. Their awareness of these is so clear and complete that the abolition of spatial and temporal distance would not have the slightest effect on their profound and categorical faith.

Furthermore, the Prophets acquire a steely determination as a result of their strivings and unstinting self-sacrifice and their continuous orientation to the origin of being; they have no fear of the problems and difficulties that confront them on the road to establishing justice and truth, and they devote their entire beings to winning the satisfaction of God. This, too, is a powerful factor in bestowing inerrancy on those men of God and protecting them from making use of their ability to sin and even from allowing the idea of sin to enter the pure sanctuary of their minds.

This comprehensive protection against sin is, then, the direct result of their encompassing knowledge of the requital that evil deeds earn and their perfect awareness of the exalted station of the Lord. It is, too, an indication of their lofty, proud spirituality which harnesses all the rebellious inclinations of their being as that they never step beyond the bounds that have been set.

Let us set aside for the moment the case of the Prophets. In every age there have been persons of pure heart who as a result of a fundamental change in their manner of thought and constant struggle against various forms of captivity, have torn apart the chains of attachment and liberated their thoughts and their deeds from the entrammeling prison of enslavement to the world. For human beings such as these, the only source of value in life has been their love for God, their determination to do His will and to advance towards Him. Their burning love, arising from their purity of mind and their belief in the primacy and authenticity of religion, gives them a certain kind of protection against many forms of sin and moral corruption.

In many cases, they may not be fully aware of the harmful consequences of sin, but their sense of obedience to God creates such a transformation in their consciousness that it functions like an impenetrable barrier interposed between them and sin. So firm and unbreakable is that barrier that instinctual desire and arbitrary inclination are unable to breach it.

Muhammad b. Umary relates the following: "I asked Hisham, the outstanding student of Imam Sadiq, peace be upon him, whether the Imams have the station of inerrancy. He answered that they do. I then asked him to explain for me the nature of their inerrancy. He replied as follows: 'There are several qualities that give rise to sin and vice: greed, envy, lust and anger, and none of these can penetrate the beings of the Imams. How might they experience greed, considering the abundant resources they have at their disposal, including the public treasury of the Muslims? Similarly, why should the Imam be envious? The envious person is the one who cannot endure the thought of someone being higher than him, and the imamate is assuredly the highest of all stations.

"As far as worldly matters are concerned, it is impossible for the Imam to be angry because he has been entrusted with the implementation of the penalties God has decreed. As for anger in matters touching on the hereafter, which is a praiseworthy form of anger, it is impossible for the Imam to fall prey to lust and desire, for he is well aware that the pleasures and desirable things of this world are transitory and totally insignificant when compared to the Divine reward and bounty which are reserved on the Day of Judgment for the pure and the worshippers of God."[12]

There are then two basic sources for the commission of sin: a failure to recognize the ugliness of sin, and a defeat of the intelligence when confronted by the power and pressure of lusts. So if a person be fully aware of the corrupt and ugly nature of all sin and if he can bring his desires fully under control, it is impossible that he should pollute his hands with the commission of sin.

Imam Sadiq, upon whom be peace, says: "God extends His aid and assistance to human beings in proportion to their will, determination and choice, so that whoever makes a correct choice and a firm determination will receive the full aid of God, and he who falls short in his choices will find God's aid withheld from him in due proportion."[13]

But as for total protection from error and sin, this is possible only through the special favor of God. The Quran says: "*Were God's mercy and favor not to embrace you, a group of enemies would have attempted to turn you aside from the right path. But through God's favor, they were able only to turn themselves aside from the right path, and they could not harm you in any way. God has bestowed on you this book and the station of wisdom and prophethood and taught you what you knew not, because God's favor and grace toward you are infinite.*" (4:113)

In addition, it can perhaps be said that the Prophets participated directly in the unfolding of realities and when the human being confronts objective realities in accordance with a certain particular sense, error and sin can have no meaning for that person. It is only when the human being attempts to transpose mental forms into objective reality that error can arise, not when the person is inwardly linked with the reality of being, a condition which makes it impossible for mistakes to occur. Thus it is that the Prophet is immune against error when guiding human beings and summoning them to God. Were it to be otherwise, you would look with doubt and hesitation on whatever the Prophet said in promulgating the commandments of God and you would not regard yourself as obliged to obey them.

Inerrancy applies to the receipt of revelation, the preservation of revelation, and the promulgation of the message. All three aspects are contained in this verse of the Noble Quran: "*In order that God might know that the Messengers have fully conveyed to mankind the messages of their Lord, that He be fully aware of what the Messengers possess and that He know full well the numbering of all things in this world...*" (38:28)

In addition, as far as the receipt of revelation is concerned, we know that all things are at the disposal of God; there is no question of any personal view being intermingled in it. We know that the infinite knowledge and power of the Creator are utterly removed from the possibility of error, and that God's complete vigilance in ensuring the propagation of His message removes the possibility of all error and mistake. So just as the receipt of God's commandments takes place beneath His vigilance, so too does the propagation of the message.

Comprehensive inerrancy, with respect to thought, word and deed, is then indispensable for undertaking the mission of guidance and leadership. It is inconceivable that God should send Messengers subject to error who would thwart the whole purpose of the message they bear.

Freedom from various bodily defects and spiritual inadequacies also forms part of the conditions of prophethood and the receipt of revelation. Contagious diseases, belonging to a family of ill-repute, a harsh and abrasive character, are some of the factors that might arouse repulsion and cause people to shun the Messenger and become disinclined toward him. Thus the aim of the Prophet's message, the training and edification of the human being, would receive a setback.

Given the fact that the Prophet is the bearer of a Divine message, the doctrines he presents must not contradict the firm principles of human logic and knowledge. Were this not to be the case, the message brought by a claimant to prophethood would not be worth studying, nor would it be necessary to demand miracles and proofs in support of it. We see, however, that the Prophet is described in certain religious traditions as 'the external intellect,' i.e., the intellect external to one's own being.

Of course, the principle we have put forward concerns the firm rules and established laws of reason and science, a category that does not include hypotheses and theories. The teachings of the Prophets are none other than that system of law laid down by the Creator, and the universal order of creation consists of scientific principles and laws. Since both orders derive from the same source, they must everywhere preserve their harmony. It is impossible that a Prophet be chosen by God and then propagate in his message something contrary to rational laws, for God Who Himself established reason as a criterion for distinguishing between the true and the false will never promulgate a commandment contradicting it. It is likewise impossible that the ordinances of heaven should contradict science, which is, in its essence, the order that God causes to rule over things. However, it should be borne in mind that if science posits a way for reaching the goal, this does not mean that the way of science is the only way available or that all others are closed.

In matters that are apparently opposed to science, one should always be cautious and avoid hasty judgments aimed at reconciling religious ordinances with scientific concerns. Science still has an infinite road to travel and there is always the possibility that scientific theories will fall subject to doubt as a result of more extensive and comprehensive research.

Lesson Nine
The Splendor of the Prophet of Islam

Previous Prophets mentioned some of the characteristics of the Prophet of Islam in their heavenly books, giving their followers the glad tidings of his future appearance. As the Quran says: *"Those to whom We sent books (the Jews and the Christians) know well of Muhammad and his truthfulness, just as they know their own children, but some of them obstinately hide the truth, although they are well aware of it."* (2:145)

In the troubled world of those days, cultural and moral decline, together with polytheism and idolatry and all their ramifications had submerged the whole globe. Even the heavenly religions that had followers in different parts of the world had undergone radical change in the course of time; not only had they lost all vitality and ability to guide mankind, but their most creative elements had fallen prey to decline. There was no hope of infusing a new spirit of life in them, of making blood course once again through their hardened arteries.

The People of the Book were therefore waiting for some profound eruption and the emergence of a new heavenly personality who would bear on his capable shoulders the heavy burden of guiding mankind, leading them away from decaying systems of thought to a new and progressive teaching.

The world had reached the end of its tether in the midst of all that confusion and unrest. It longed for a whole new environment, different from the poisoned one in which it lived, and waited for a hand to emerge from the sleeve of the unseen which would destroy the crumbling structure of the old order and build a new one on its ruins.

Each of the peoples and nations that were then dominating the world had in some way fallen prey to anarchy and confusion. The

Arabs who lived at the crossroads of the great powers of that age and whose broad homeland was traversed by the caravans of international commerce felt more powerfully each day their weakness and impotence vis-a-vis their powerful neighbors. The danger of complete extinction that faced the Arabs because of their lack of an organized political structure and because of the power of their oppressive neighbors, was plain to any farsighted person.

It was under these circumstances that the promised deliverer Muhammad, upon whom be peace, was born at dawn on Friday, the seventeenth day of the month of Rabi' al-Awwal, fifty three years before the migration (*hijra*), corresponding to the year 570 of the Christian era, in the city of Mecca in the Arabian Peninsula. It was a land of stifling repression, the very symbol of a sick and decadent society where ignorance was actively cultivated. It was like a swamp where the waters of corruption stagnated, a pit in which humanity had been buried.

It was in such a place that the Prophet first set eyes on the world and the light of his splendor first shone on the horizons of human life; it was there that this quintessence of being who was destined to bring human thought to maturity generated a new energy and an inexhaustible vitality in mankind.

None could reach his level of excellence in the qualities he possessed, and all expectations were fulfilled with his coming. He appeared at a time that society was prepared for him because it needed him. Not only the Arabian peninsula but the world at large was prepared for his coming, because the whole of the ancient world was longing with all of its being for the appearance of a man who would take it by the hand and guide it to its goal.

The sphere of the heavens, in its prolonged and ceaseless rotation had never been able to bring forth a creature like him whose substance was pure and free of all defect, who was completely untainted by all imperfection. History bears witness that this blessed infant, whose splendor shone forth from the arms of his mother, Aminah, over the whole world, came to establish the most creative of all faiths and the purest, most profound and pervasive of impetus, for the cultivation of knowledge and spirituality.

By prohibiting flattery and subservience before the thrones of the emperors and the powerful, he awakened to new life the dormant minds of human beings and created a suitable environment for their cultivation. He drove away idols from the threshold of their veneration, instructing them instead in the mysteries of Divine unity and teaching them how to live and die with dignity.

As a result of his teachings, idolatry gave way to monotheism and the worship of the one true God; ignorance yielded to knowledge and science, brotherliness, compassion, and other human virtues took the place of hostility, hatred and discord; and those who had been reared in an atmosphere of corruption and ignorance became the choicest specimens of humanity.

Abdullah, the father of the Prophet, was a descendent of Ishmael. His was a truly human heart, a heart that overflowed with love, fidelity and mercy. After marrying Aminah, he went trading in Syria, accompanying a caravan that was leaving Mecca. Aminah was already pregnant and impatiently awaited the return of her husband. But a severe illness laid hold of Abdullah, drawing the life out of him so that he died far away from his homeland.

He closed his eyes on the world and its pleasures, full of painful regret that he would be unable to see Aminah again or the child that she was to bear him. After a time, the young mother learned that in the sixteenth year of her life she had been widowed and left alone with a small infant.

Her father-in-law, Abd al-Mutallib, took her and the infant to his own house, and then decided to send his newborn grandson to the Banu Sa'd in the desert, to be suckled by them and to grow up in the pure air of the desert.

Four months had passed after the birth of the Most Noble Prophet when the wetnurses of the Banu Sa'd came to Mecca and one of them, a woman of pure disposition called Halimah, declared herself ready to suckle the orphaned Muhammad.[14]

Halimah returned to the desert with the child to take care of him there and he stayed among the Banu Sa'd continuing to grow until he was weaned. Still, however, his grandfather continued to leave him in the care of the tribe until he was five years old, and throughout this period the kindly wetnurse took good care of him and paid attention to his upbringing. He learned the best and most authentic dialect of Arabic, and imbibed the most eloquent forms of Arabic speech. Halimah took him to see his mother two or three times, and on the last of these occasions she turned him over to his mother. When a year had passed, Aminah left Mecca, taking him with her to show him to the wetnurses who lived in the villages between Mecca and Yathrib. Full of joyous satisfaction, she reached the dwelling places of the wetnurses, but she was not destined to return to Mecca.

Aminah died in the course of her return journey and was buried where she died. Her infant orphaned son, now six years of age, was left alone at the side of her grave.[15]

He had never seen his father nor had he fully enjoyed the kindness and affection of his mother for just as he was about to begin benefiting from her upbringing, fate snatched her away and left him alone in the awesome expanse of the desert.

At the time of the death of his mother, the infant Prophet had reached the age when intellectual and spiritual characteristics begin to develop. His grandfather, Abd al-Mutallib, for whom he was the only reminder of his own son, Abdullah, and a source of consolation for his weary heart, then assumed responsibility for his care and fulfilled this trust worthily until his death.

This period in which the Prophet enjoyed the care and protection of his grandfather, which were like a soothing balm placed on his wounds, did not last long. Just as he reached the age of eight, the life of Abd al-Mutallib came to an end. A new grief assailed the Prophet, lines of sorrow and pain became apparent in his face, and the powerful spirit that was never troubled by the perils he faced throughout his life was gripped by the pain of bereavement.

However, Divine favor had bestowed on him the ability to accept and endure these setbacks. For an orphan who was due to become the father of humanity and the comforter of all the burdened and oppressed in the world had to become acquainted, from childhood onward, with all forms of deprivation and affliction; he had to have a spirit as firm and resistant as a mountain in order to carry on his shoulders the otherwise unbearable burden of the Divine message. The ability to resist and withstand all kinds of obstacles and difficulties was essential for him, and his lofty and expansive spirit was a sign that he possessed precisely this ability.

The orphaned boy next moved to the house of his paternal uncle, Abu Talib, a great and noble person who was the full brother of his father. Although he was surrounded by the kindness of his cousins in his uncle's house, Muhammad, upon whom be peace, naturally felt lonely.

One morning he learned that his uncle Abu Talib was planning to journey to Syria, leaving him behind. Muhammad, upon whom be peace, then approached his uncle and asked him for permission to accompany him, but his uncle refused, since he was still too young to endure the rigors of travel.

When the caravan was about to depart, Muhammad's eyes filled with tears, and Abu Talib was deeply moved by the sad expression on his face. He was compelled to take him with him on his journey to Syria, and thus it was that at the age of twelve he set out on a journey to distant lands.

Before the Quraysh caravan reached its destination, it passed through the city of Bostra where the party met a monk called Buhayra. Buhayra passed his days engaged in devotion in his cell, and being a man deeply learned in Christianity, he was revered by all of the Christians.

As soon as Buhayra caught sight of Abu Talib's nephew, he found himself profoundly attracted by him. His piercing and mysterious glances seemed to indicate some secret hidden in his heart. Finally Buhayra broke his silence and asked to whom this child belonged. The party pointed to his uncle, and Abu Talib said, "This is my nephew." Buhayra then said: "This child has a brilliant future in front of him. This is the promised Messenger whose coming and prophethood have been foretold in the scriptures, and I see in his person all the signs mentioned in those books. He is that true Prophet whose name and family I have read of. I know where this great personality will rise to fame and how the Divine religion he brings will conquer the whole world. However, you must conceal him from the view of the Jews, because they will destroy him once they become aware of this." [16]

Historians have clearly discerned in all dimensions of his person great spiritual energy and power, together with all the other qualities that are fitting in a great leader sent by heaven.

No researcher or scholar can claim that the Prophet, upon whom be peace, fell prey at any point in his life to moral or spiritual deviation or to nervous excitement. Although the characteristics of the Prophet of Islam are more clearly and fully known than those of other people who have left their mark on history, in the near or distant past, history cannot point to the slightest rebelliousness, ill-temper or evil conduct on his part, nor even to a single error or sin.

The remarkable life of the exalted Prophet of Islam is clearly and completely known in all of its aspects: the period before his birth, his infancy, his youth, his moral characteristics, his travels, his marriages, his conduct in war and peace.

Recorded history bears witness that the slightest trace of corrupt belief cannot be found to have clouded his brilliant visage. Although he had no access to any form of instruction, he had no connection with the Age of Ignorance surrounding him, and vice was never able to take root in him.

The creedal environment in which he grew up was a compound of polytheism and idolatry, as is shown by the strong resistance of the Arabs to his summons to monotheism. The entirety of his early life was spent in the midst of an ignorant, evil-living and oppressive people and he never left that environment before the beginning of his mission with the exception of two journeys outside the Arabian Peninsula, once in childhood, in the company of Abu Talib, in the early part of the second decade of his life, and once in his mid-thirties when he went trading with the goods of Khadijah. Nonetheless, we find not the least affinity between his personality and the society in which he lived.

The aspect of his personality that was particularly valuable in that corrupt and polluted environment was his honesty, trustworthiness and unfailing sense of justice, together with his hostility to all the forms of humiliation from which mankind was suffering.

Muhammad, upon whom be peace, captivated the hearts of his contemporaries with his nobility of character and his kindness toward the weak and the afflicted. Friend and enemy are agreed that none of the men of his age even approached him in the perfection of his attributes and spiritual characteristics.

For example, Zayd b. Haritha, who had been separated from his family at an early age and was given by Khadijah to the most Noble Messenger, upon whom be peace, as a slave, spent his entire life with him. After a time, Zayd's father came looking for him in order to reclaim him. Now Zayd had been emancipated by the Prophet, upon whom be peace, but he was still a slave to the love, the greatness and the splendor of the Prophet, and captivated by the excellence of his conduct and behavior. So although he was free to return to his family, he preferred to remain with the Prophet and serve him.

Eloquence and profundity of speech, fairness in judging, superior intelligence and perception, heavenly disposition and brilliance of thought—all these were abundantly evident in the being of this great personage. They shone forth in all the varied scenes of his life, and he so lived that years before the beginning of his prophetic mission, he was awarded the title *amin*, 'trustworthy', an eloquent description of his whole mode of conduct.[17]

During one of the religious festivals of the Quraysh, an incident occurred that struck a blow at the rule of the idolators. In the middle of the festival, while the people were gathered around an idol and rubbing their foreheads in the dust in front of it, a few clear-minded and pure-hearted people such as Waraqa b. Nawfal, who were distressed by the corruption prevailing in Mecca, began to discuss the situation. They asked themselves how much longer it could continue and when the time of delivery would come. Why were those people prostrating in front of objects, and why had they distorted the religion of their forefather Abraham?

One of the things they said was this: "What is that piece of stone around which they are walking? A thing that neither sees nor hears, that does not breathe, that can give no benefit and inflict no harm!"[18]

As the Prophet grew into maturity of the body and mind, he became inclined to periodic retreat and withdrawal. His profound inward thoughts, together with the unsuitability of his environment, impelled him to seek solitude.

In his evaluation of phenomena he was never hasty nor dependent on his own ideas and perceptions. He clearly saw a hand that inscribed its will on the pages of nature, and this was itself an indication of the profoundity of his vision and the exaltation of his thought.

He would spend the month of Ramadan alone in the cave of Hira, on the outskirts of Mecca, benefitting fully from the darkness and silence. Far removed from men and their corruption, he engaged in supplication and armed himself with the weapon of faith. He developed his spiritual personality through humble worship in the presence of the Majestic Creator that enveloped his whole being, and through cultivating the thoughts that welled up from the depths of his spirit. In the morning, overflowing with faith and certainty, with spiritual enthusiasm and vigor, he would leave the cave to engage in his daily tasks.

Love of God animated his kind and tranquil face, and he was greatly distressed by the polytheism and foolishness of his people who would prostrate before the idols they had manufactured themselves. He began to struggle against this idolatry, remaining steadfast in the truth through all the trials and hardships he underwent.

As his age approached forty, signs of anxiety and distress became marked in his behavior and speech, and he told his loving wife of sounds that were continually re-echoing in his ear and of a dazzling light that would envelop him.

Lesson Ten
Beginning of the Mission

Finally the appointed moment arrived, the moment which had been foretold by previous Prophets to their followers. At the age of forty, the orphan son of Abdullah attained the exalted station of messengerhood. It was he alone that time had prepared for guiding the world with his message for only this great and heavy responsibility could call for such qualities and virtues as he possessed. Only in such a vast enterprise could the energies of that quintessence of all existence unfold, for the entire being of Muhammad, upon whom be peace, was prepared to undertake the grave task of prophethood. If he had not been prepared, in the best possible way, to assume that sacred and fateful responsibility, there would have been none other in the world capable of conveying the Divine mission in all its dimensions. It was only the being of Muhammad, upon whom be peace, that was capable of stilling the thirst of the world.

While engaged in worship in a corner of the cave of Hira in the heart of the night, the Prophet who had never studied or attended a school, was suddenly shaken by the summons, "O Muhammad!" followed by the command to recite, this being the beginning of revelation. A wave arose from the limitless ocean of Divinity, rent the breast of the Prophet, bewildered and anxious, and filled to the brim the cup of his spirit.

The shining of a light from the realm of the unseen covered and enveloped his being and shone forth on his fair features, giving rise to new and bright life in the darkness of the night. Then, with a painful tumult in his heart and bearing on his shoulders the heaviest responsibility conceivable, he set out for home from the cave of Hira, destined to become the teacher of all human beings and to assume the leadership of humanity on its long march forward.

What force was it that had disquieted him despite his infinite patience, made him anxious despite all his tranquil courage, and plunged his whole being into painful turmoil? Thereafter the envoy of revelation came repeatedly, reciting verses to him, profound and astounding verses that bore no resemblance from the point of view of style and content either to the words of the Prophet himself, eloquent as they were, or to the conventional prose and poetry of the age.

Although the Arabs of the Age of Ignorance knew neither how to read nor how to write and had no historians, philosophers or scholars, they were famed for the excellence of their poetry and the eloquence of their speech. The Prophet, however, had never participated before the beginning of his mission in the cultivation of the arts of poetry and eloquence.

His conduct, on the one hand, and the verses of the Quran, on the other, both testify that he made no compromises in conveying his message. He conveyed the message that he had been ordered to deliver clearly, unambiguously and in utter contradiction both with the beliefs and inclinations of the people and with his own immediate interests. He loudly proclaimed the revelation he had received to the evil and the ignorant, to a people made degenerate and corrupt by the worship of the idols they had fashioned themselves, and he informed them that their sole salvation lay in the worship of the One God.

The new factor that appeared at a particular time in the life of the Prophet and caused him to engage in unprecedented forms of activity was the wondrous phenomenon of revelation, the heavenly message which he as the most lofty and qualified of men had been chosen to receive. Before then, no preliminary effort or particular inclination had been seen on his part that might have led to the bringing about of the sudden and remarkable transformation of the world he was now about to accomplish.

The factor that had this profound effect on Muhammad, that changed that quiet and reflective man into an explosive source of revolutionary energy and enabled him to bring about such a profound transformation of humanity, from within the intense darkness of the Arabs' Age of Ignorance, was nothing other than revelation. It was a call that penetrated the very depths of the souls of human beings that melted the marrow of their bones, and directed all their strivings to the attainment of perfection.

The command of revelation negated all the false and lying criteria which human beings had regarded as the measure of goodness and considered the sole means of evaluating human characteristics and habits, while, in fact, clothing falsehood in the garment of truth. It brought into operation new and clear criteria which showed human beings the goals to which they should strive to advance and brought about creativity in their lives. The veil of ignorance and silence was torn apart, the human beings' energies were set to work, the power of thought within them was aroused, and their spirits were borne aloft toward the infinite summit of being.

A people who in their ignorance and lowliness would tear each apart on account of the most insignificant things and had lost all virtue, thanks to their various forms of enslavement, now became, through Islam and its great concept of monotheism—the true pillar of humanity and the breaker of idols—so elevated of spirit and so self-sacrificing that they happily abandoned both their lives and their property. The remarkable stories of self-sacrifice on the part of those early Muslims will stand eternally as examples of true nobility.

The Prophet of Islam had the vision and belief of a world leader, but he began to proclaim his Divine summons to monotheism in a relatively restricted sphere, a closed environment where tribal institutions exercised great influence and idols were counted as the most sacred and beloved of objects. It was an environment that was not in any way prepared to accept the message of Divine unity.

The heavenly teachings of Islam and the culture to which they gave rise were superior not only to the intellectual atmosphere prevailing in the idolatrous society of the Arabs but also to all the religious doctrines and cultures of that age.

The program for reforming systems of thought and culture that had become corrupt was laid down by a man who had never studied, who was unlettered, and who knew nothing of the religious books or the civilization of his age.

At first he invited his relatives to worship the Creator, and then the people of Mecca and the Arabian Peninsula. Finally he proclaimed to the entire world his mission as the last of the Prophets.

Ali b. Abi Talib, upon whom be peace, was the first man to accept his religion,[19] and his wife, Khadijah, was the first woman to believe in his heavenly mission. Gradually others, too, proclaimed their belief in the new religion.

Ali, upon whom be peace, said: "One day the Prophet summoned his relatives and addressed them as follows: 'Children of Abd al-Mutallib! I bring you something more excellent than anything the Arabs have ever brought you. I bring you as a gift the means of your salvation in this world and the hereafter, a Divine Command to which I invite your submission. Which among you will help me, so that he will be my brother, my successor and my legatee among you?'

"All remained silent but I, who was younger than all of them, said: 'O Messenger of God, I will help you!' Muhammad, upon whom be peace, then said: 'This is my brother, my successor and my legatee among you; listen to this words and accept them.' "[20]

With his extraordinary powers of leadership and mature political sense, the Prophet began to refashion human beings by concentrating on their inner beings. He strove to awaken the sense of monotheism that was innate in them by drawing their attention to the mysteries of creation and acquainting them with the infiniteness of the universe.

The Prophet had been born into an environment where human beings engaged in empty boasting out of their shortsightedness and tribal mentality, where privileges were based on unjust social conditions and prejudices. Now he arose and swept aside all those false privileges. He established new values and concepts with respect to labor, life and social relations, in the framework of a series of rules and ordinances, and strove to concentrate all the goals and thoughts of the human being on a program for liberating peoples from slavery, and delivering the oppressed from the tyranny of emperors and kings. Even for those who do not regard these exalted aims as having a heavenly origin will admit that they are among the most exalted and previous values observable in human history.

The preaching of the Prophet remained hidden for three years. He established Islam secretly. Throughout the thirteen years that he concentrated his mission on Mecca, the leaders of the polythe-

ists, who understood well the gravity of their situation, resisted
him with obstinate hostility, doing their utmost to preserve the
beliefs and customs of the Age of Ignorance and to silence the
liberating cry of Islam. They conducted themselves with extreme
ferocity against all who had converted to Islam.

They fettered and chained those defenseless ones for their
crime of having accepted Islam and left them lying hungry and
thirsty on the ground beneath the burning sun of Mecca. They
placed heavy stones on their bare breasts in an effort to make them
foreswear the religion of Muhammad. Yasir and Sumayyah, those
two heroes, were subjected to the most barbaric of torturers and
every day endured the weight of the heavy stones the Quraysh
used to place on their breasts beneath the fiery rays fo the sun.
These were the first martyrs of Islam: the husband died under
torture and the wife was martyred by Abu Jahl.[21]

By applying these methods, the idolaters wanted to stifle Islam
while it was still in the cradle. For it was a life and death struggle:
if the call of the Prophet were to advance, they would lose forever
their sovereignty and the empty privileges they had enjoyed.
Envy, too, played an important role in intensifying their hostility to
Islam.

The continuation of this unpleasant situation turned the city of
Mecca into a prison and a place of torture for the defenceless
Muslims. The polytheists made it forbidden even to listen to the
verses of the Quran, and they appointed certain people to go out
and meet incoming caravans and warn them not to make contact
with the Muslims.

Because of the pressure and cruelty of the Quraysh, a number
of Muslims decided to leave Mecca and migrate to Ethiopia, in
order to have there a safe and tranquil environment in which to
practice their religion, and worship the One God, free from harassment by the unbelievers.

Even then the opponents of Islam did not abandon their
persecution of them. The Quraysh sent two envoys to the ruler of
Ethiopia in order to persuade him to send back the Muslims. But
the ruler received the migrants hospitably and extended his protection to them, so that they were able to carry out their devotional
duties in freedom in the land of Ethiopia. When the envoys of
Quraysh presented gifts to the Emperor in an effort to have the

refugees sent back to Mecca, he answered that since they had chosen him out of all rulers which whom to seek refuge, he could not expel them without first investigating them.

When Ja'far b. Abi Talib, the spokesman of the migrants, spoke of the beliefs of the Muslims concerning Jesus, upon whom be peace, the Emperor was much impressed and said: "I swear by God that Jesus had no station beyond what these Muslim say."

Although the corrupt ministers of the Emperor were displeased by his words, he praised the beliefs of the Muslims and gave them complete freedom, turning over to them the gifts that the Qurayshi envoys had brought. He said that when God had given him power, He had not required any bribe of him, and that it was therefore inappropriate that he should now benefit from such gifts.[22]

Thus light triumphed over darkness, and the forces of polytheism and ignorance retreated in   defeat and despair.

The Tactics of the Enemy

When the enemies of Islam saw that their power was crumbling in the face of the new order of monotheism and realized that Islam was felling all their idols, both material and mental, just like an axe felling trees, they first resorted to threats. When they saw that threats were useless, they tried by means of promises and the award of privileges to turn the Prophet back from the path on which he had embarked.

But these efforts, too, proved fruitless as he rejected with disgust all their promises of power and wealth, with all the firmness demanded of the bearer of a heavenly mission. He proclaimed: "I swear by God that if you were to put the sun in my right hand and the moon in my left, I would never abandon my mission until the religion of God spreads over the globe or I lose my life in propagating it."[23]

Ya'qubi writes as follows in his history: "The Quraysh told Abu Talib that his nephew was vilifying their gods, accusing them of insanity and proclaiming that their ancestors were in error. They asked him to tell the Prophet that they would give him all of their wealth if he would abandon his preaching. Muhammad, upon whom be peace, answered: 'God did not raise me up as a Prophet in order that I might accumulate the wealth of this world; rather, He raised me up to convey His message to mankind and to call men to Him.'"[24]

Then the enemy changed its tactics once more, and employed every conceivable weapon against this movement in order to destroy the newly constructed edifice of Islam.

Old enemies made peace with each other in order to destroy the Prophet. By attempting to blacken the fair name of the Prophet and sully his reputation, they wished both to quench the fire of hatred they felt in their hearts and to neutralize his summons and call.

Everywhere they proclaimed that he was a magician, a sorcerer, a madman, a poet, and they stirred up the ignorant against him. This is the same satanic strategy that the enemies of truth always use in order to undermine and defeat great personalities.

The Quran makes it plain that this strategy was not peculiar to the Age of the Prophet of Islam. It proclaims: *"Never was a Prophet raised up for earlier peoples without men saying that he was a sorcerer or mad. Is this a legacy of denial they have transmitted from one age to the next? No, these people are themselves rebellious and transgressors."* (51:52-53)

The Prophet, however, consistently refrained from adopting an attitude of anger toward his enemies. Although their fanatical prejudice, their shortsightedness, their blind traditionalism, and their calumnies increased the difficulties that he was facing, they were never able to arouse his anger. Instead, he sought always to bring them to see the truth, by means of spiritual instruction.

Neither pressure nor promises, neither deprivation nor difficulty, were able to shake the determination of the Prophet. Nor did the spreading of cunning and baseless accusations yield any result, for the compelling logic of the Quran and its re-echoing melody were too profound and too exalted not to leave an effect on the mind of whoever heard it; or to captivate and transform them. Even enemies were sometimes compelled to admit the truth.

Tabarsi writes in his commentary on the Quran: "When Walid, the celebrated sage of the Arabs, heard the Prophet recite the verses of *Surah Fussilat,* he was profoundly affected. The Banu Makhzum gathered around him and he described the Quran to them as follows: 'It has a distinctive charm and a unique beauty. Its branches are laden with fruit and roots are blessed. It is an elevated form of speech, higher than all others.' Thus he spoke and went on his way, and the Quraysh thought he had embraced the religion of Muhammad, upon whom be peace."[25]

Although the Prophet had vast resources of patience, he was sometimes distressed by the foolish conduct of his people. He would go into a corner until Divine command summoned him back to his grave responsibilities, for to desist for a single instant in striving toward the sacred goals that had been set for him was impermissible; he had to shun all rest and retreat. (See 74:1-4)

One of the distinctive factors enabling the Prophets to succeed in the movements they launched was their steadfastness and power of endurance. The Quran mentions the method followed by the Prophets in their struggles as follows: *"Ishmael, Idris and Dhu 'l-Kifl were all steadfast and patient in fulfilling their missions."* (21:98)

All the envoys of God endured hardship and suffering when they were faced with denial and rejection, but they remained steadfast until the aid of God secured them their triumph.

Lesson Eleven
The Beginning of Migration

As a result of the oppressive atmosphere in Mecca and the un-bridled persecution of the Muslims that threatened them con-stantly with imprisonment, torture and death, and in recognition of the fact that the Muslim warriors were not yet ready for battle, the command was given to migrate. The Prophet gave instructions that the Muslims leave the city one by one and proceed to Yathrib.

The Quraysh understood well the danger this represented, and they stooped to all kinds of illicit means to prevent the Companions of the Prophet from departing, even taking their wives hostage. But true to their original decision, the Muslims began gradually to leave the center of polytheism, ignorance and oppression, leaving behind their attachments and their families in order to migrate. The people of Yathrib took them into their embrace.

Most of the Muslims had left, and Mecca was almost empty. This unusual situation and the disquieting news arriving from Medina greatly worried the Quraysh. Since the previous ill con-duct of the leaders of unbelief and rejection had not yielded any results, they arrived at a grave and perilous decision: they planned to kill the Prophet. It was agreed that as soon as night fell, the designated assassins should go about their work.[26]

They surrounded the house of the Prophet at night, waiting in front of the door for the Prophet to emerge at dawn. They kept his room under surveillance throughout the night and were convinced that the son of Abdullah, who had not a single protector in the city, would be unable to escape their siege of his house and that his fate would be sealed at dawn.

However, the Messenger of God ordered Ali, upon whom be peace, to sleep in his bed—Ali whose very spirit had been formed in Islam and who thought nothing of dying for the sake of God and the life of the Prophet. The Prophet then left the house secretly, in the company of Abu Bakr.

At this point a man chanced by the house and asked those who were thirsting for the blood of the Messenger of God whom they were waiting for. When they replied, "Muhammad," he told them, "he has escaped your grasp." When dawn rended the breast of the horizons, they were astonished to see Ali, upon whom be peace, rise up from the bed of the Prophet.

It is not quite clear how the Prophet managed to break through the circle that had been thrown round his house without arousing attention. What is certain is that God had willed to deliver His chosen Messenger from the grasp of those vile and lowly persons.

The Prophet left Mecca in the heart of the night and took refuge in a cave, and then continued on to Medina using back roads. Once he reached the city, it was clear that the treacherous plan of the Quraysh had ultimately harmed them and benefited Islam and the Muslims. The powerful hand that had protected the burning torch of Islam for thirteen years against all harm was able with ease to bring this conspiracy to nought.

Before the migration of the Prophet, a number of citizens of Medina had come to Mecca to seek the support of the Quraysh in the tribal wars that for years had pitted the Aws against the Khazraj. Despite the warnings of the Quraysh, they had listened to the words of the Prophet, upon whom be peace, and had been deeply affected, even transformed, by them. The next time that they came to Mecca in order to perform the pilgrimage, they had formally accepted the summons of the Messenger of God and embraced Islam. After leaving Mecca and returning to their native city, they expended great efforts to enlighten the people of Yathrib and convey the Divine message to all classes of the population. This represented in itself a massive blow to the foundations of idolatry.

The people of Medina were exhausted by the long tribal wars, and they saw in the call of the Messenger a message of hope and a means of deliverance from the consuming fire of civil strife. In order to appreciate the need of society at that time for the great movement of Islam and to grasp the role played by Islam in putting an end to corruption and misguidance, we must understand the situation prevailing in the Arabian Peninsula.

Ali, upon whom be peace, said: "God sent Muhammad, upon whom be peace and blessings, to warn people away from the path in which they were engaged, and He appointed him trustee of His heavenly decrees. At that time, O Arabs, you aware following the worst of beliefs and customs, and you lived in the most deprived of all lands. You slept in the midst of rough stones and poisonous snakes, drank foul water, ate no proper food, split each other's blood, disregarded the ties of kinship. There were idols among you, and sin had rendered you impotent."[27]

The migration of the Most Noble Messenger to Medina, which marked the beginning of the Islamic era, was the start of a new chapter in the history of Islam. Thereafter blows rained down continuously on the forces of corruption and falsehood.

The Prophet's cause took root in Medina. His call went from house to house, and a new society crystallized. The powerful logic and creativity of the ideas set forth by Muhammad, upon whom be peace and blessings, were such that the previous cultural, moral and social structures of the people of Medina thoroughly collapsed, together with all the customs that dominated their lives. The chains of slavery and the fetters of cruelty and oppression were torn asunder; the powerful were pulled down from their thrones of arrogance. The immortal *shari'a* brought by the Prophet to mankind as a gift of new norms of justice and elevated culture, and Medina became swiftly transformed into a religious, social and military base for the Islamic cause.

The experiences they had gone through in Mecca, the continued harassment and torture of the believers, the sundering of old ties and the forging of new ones, the continuous deepening of spiritual maturity—all this contributed to the development of the migrants, so that just as Medina became a center of spiritual and political power for the whole of Arabia, so, too, it became a base for the ultimate diffusion of Islam throughout the world.

It was from there that the Prophet of Islam presented his message to the nations of the world. He summoned all human beings to unite beneath the banner of monotheism and its vital, life-giving teachings, so that in less than half a century the religion he had founded brought under its sway the great and prosperous nations of that day. It fell like a rain of mercy and blessing on souls and hearts that were anxious to receive it.

Those who fail to grasp the profound causes of events attribute the swift progress and diffusion of Islam to mere chance. In fact, none of the major events of the world can be attributed to chance, and this is especially true of the emergence of the founder of an ethical, philosophical and legal system.

Can it have been a matter of pure accident that the spark of such a phenomenon should have appeared but once in the history of Arabia, without anything similar occurring there ever again.

If certain sociological factors caused the emergence in Arabia of such a vast movement, why should another hero comparable to the Prophet not have arisen in the same area, because of the same factors? Why should this one particular event stand forth from all others, as a unique and self-contained instance?

If a revolutionary movement occurs in a given society as the product of certain social conditions, it is impossible that it should happen suddenly, without any precedent or connection to prior developments. On the contrary, it is like a wave that gradually expands, until the conditions become fully ripe for the emergence of a leader.

When propagating his message, the Prophet of Islam did not represent the latest in a chain of ideological movements such as occur in every society. No groundwork had been laid, in the environment where he grew up, for the lofty concepts, values and ideas that he presented nor did any foundation exist on which he might have built.

The revolutionary wave of Islam derived its force exclusively from the being of the Prophet; it came about without any preliminary. It was not a question of the revolutionary movement, comprising the Companions of the Prophet, serving as a nucleus around which the message grew; on the contrary, that movement was itself an extension of the person of the Prophet. The movement was a part of his person; his person was not part of the movement. From this point of view, the revolutionary movement of the Prophet of Islam is utterly different from all other movements in history.

In Islam, we encounter a comprehensive, all-embracing movement that concerns itself with all aspects of life, for it represents a profound revolution in all human values and concepts. The teachings of Islam shook the very foundations of tribal society, and so vast and lofty was the Islamic ideal that it conceived the idea of a world society, bringing together all human beings under the banner of monotheism.

It is useful to hear these facts as others have expounded them. Nehru, for example, the well-known Indian statesman, writes as follows: "It is strange that this Arab race, which for long ages had lived a sleepy existence, apparently cut off from what was happening elsewhere, should suddenly wake up and show such tremendous energy as to startle and upset the world. The story of the Arabs, and of how they spread rapidly over Asia, Europe and Africa, and of the high culture and civilization which they developed, is one of the wonders of history.

"Islam was the new force or idea which woke up the Arabs and filled them with self-confidence and energy. This was a religion started by a new Prophet, Muhammad. Within seven years of the flight, Muhammad returned to Mecca as its master. Even before this he sent out from Medina a summons to the kings and rulers of the world to acknowledge the one God and his Prophet. Heraclius, the Constantinople Emperor, got it while he was still engaged in his campaign against the Persians in Syria; the Persian King got it; and it is said that even Tai-Tsung got it in China. They must have wondered, these kings and rulers, who this unknown person was who dared to command them! From the sending of these messages we can form some idea of the supreme confidence in himself and his mission which Muhammad must have had. And this confidence and faith he managed to give to this people, and with this to inspire and console them, this desert people of no great consequence managed to conquer half the known world.

"Confidence and faith in themselves were a great thing. Islam also gave them a message of brotherhood—of the equality of all those who were Muslims. A measure of democracy was thus placed before the people. Compared to the corrupt Christianity of the day, this message of brotherhood must have had a great appeal, not only for the Arabs, but also for the inhabitants of many countries where they went."[28]

This profound and amazing transformation in human history was originated with one man acting entirely alone. He had no material resources at his command, had never engaged in scientific or technical study, and had never even taken anything from the learning of others. This cannot be regarded as a natural or normal occurrence; it is, on the contrary, eloquent testimony to the super-human capacities of that outstanding personality.

Were his enemies in Arabia not to have engaged him in internal wars, he would have summoned other peoples to Islam more swiftly and energetically. But the unrelenting attacks of his enemies compelled him to devote the major part of his time and resources to the defense of Islam.

An Answer to the Opponents of Islam

Opponents of Islam make the criticism that Islam relied on military force in order to secure its progress. However, we see that the Prophet never initiated hostilities against any group or people, whether it be the Jews or the Quraysh or the Byzantines. History bears witness that all the wars waged by the Most Noble Messenger, upon whom be peace and blessings, were defensive in nature: the purpose was always to respond to the attacks of the enemy, with the exception of certain cases where the Muslim were convinced that the enemy would persist in its aggressiveness and treachery and were correspondingly ordered to take the initiative in defending themselves.

In the following verses from the Quran, the initial reason for legislating jihad—i.e., responding to the attacks of an aggressive enemy—is clearly laid forth: *"Permission is given to the warriors of Islam to fight against their enemies, for they have suffered oppression at their hands. God is able to aid them, and they are people who have been expelled from their homeland without due reason. Their crime was this, that they said, "God is our Lord." (22:39-40) "Fight in the way of God against those who do battle with you, but be careful not to transgress the bounds, for God loves not the transgressors." (2:190) "If they break their oath after concluding a treaty and vilify your religion, fight against the leaders of the unbelievers, for they observe no pledge or treaty; only then may they cease their violations." (9:12)*

Were the Muslims carrying weapons at the very dawn of Islam when the polytheists began turning to Islam in droves? Did the Muslims start a war in order to diffuse and propagate the religion of God? Everyone knows that in the very beginning, far from attacking any group or nation, the Muslims were themselves the victims of aggression.

Moreover, if it be supposed that the early Muslims embraced Islam without understanding its veracity, later generations were under no compulsion to follow them; it was the profundity of the Divine teachings that elicited their belief, in accordance with love, willingness and free choice.

If we assumed that Islam was imposed on people through coercion and threats, a corollary of this assumption would be that conversion to Islam was compulsory wherever Islam was strong. We see, however, that Islam gave human beings the choice of either accepting Islam or simply assenting to its governmental institutions while retaining their own religion. If Islam did not respect freedom of opinion, it would never have provided for the second possibility. Islam never took advantage of its position of strength to force people to accept the religion of God.

Apart from all this, faith and belief are a matter of the heart; they can never come into being without an inward inclination on the part of the human being, purely through the exercise of compulsion and force. In order to change the beliefs and ideas of people, instruction, teaching, deduction and logic are called for; force and coercion can never remove beliefs that have taken root in people's minds.

Islam had a recourse to military force and began an armed struggle at a time when people had been deprived of freedom of thought and denied the opportunity to choose the correct path. Islam issued its proclamation of war in order to defeat the oppressive tyrants who were preventing the Islamic call from being preached freely and to put an end to the stifling of thought. Only then would the masses of humanity be able, in an atmosphere of liberty to choose with absolute freedom a correct path in life. If Islam had not acted thus, truth would have been stifled in the cradle.

In order for the religion which has human happiness as its aim and wishes to reform all of human affairs to reach its lofty goals, and in order for those persons who have the capacity to learn and assimilate the teachings of that religion to come into contact with it, without encountering any obstacle, a position of dominance must be attained. It is obvious, moreover, that power can be defeated only by power.

In order to destroy the forces that were standing in the path of the diffusion of the light of truth and were fighting against the formation and development of sound and exalted modes of thought, does any path exist save confrontation and battle against the agents of corruption?

The obstinate chiefs of the Quraysh wished to exploit the ignorance and weakness of the people, to continue ruling over their lives, their property and their honor, and to preserve forever the customs of ignorance that underlie their hereditary rule. They could not tolerate the influence, still less the prevalence, of a religion that was seizing them by the throat and dragging them down from their thrones of arrogance and self-worship. They understood well that the spread of Islam would utterly destroy their ancient, rotting customs and all their pomp and splendor. Hence they rose up with all their beings to fight against this religion and the laws it was bringing, in a struggle the purpose of which was the defence of their ancestral customs and traditions and their hereditary lordship and rule.

Was it possible for Islam to respond to such ideas and motivations purely with logic and proof? If a certain group of people tries to place a government in difficulty, drawing the sword and lighting fires everywhere, can the government in question save itself without resort to military force? How else can it defeat the miscreants? Thus the Quran says: *"Fight against them until disorder is brought to an end and the religion of God is established. If they cease causing disorder, do not fight against them."* (2:190) No one can deny that in such cases it is a necessary final resort to take up weapons, because disorder, corruption, and violence will end only when the glint of the sword flashes and the hands of the miscreants are severed.

Islam is not, then, a religion of violence and war, nor was the Prophet of God one who sought to destroy the enemy in battle despite the availability of other means. At a time when the Muslims were being harassed and tortured by the polytheists in Mecca for the crime of having accepted Islam, a Divine command entrusted them with the duty of delivering the oppressed masses from the grasp of cruel tyrants and cleansing the surrounding area of all forms of slavery and domination, by recourse to military force. Only thus could the newly emergent Islamic society continue to grow and develop in freedom.

The Quran says: *"Why do you not rise up in jihad in the path of God and for the sake of delivering the oppressed? A group of men, women and children in Mecca are prisoners to the cruelty of the unjust, and they say: 'O Lord, deliver us from this realm of the oppressors and set us free, and send us one who will lead us and aid us.'"* (4:75)

The battle implied here is one waged against oppressors who are fighting against God, freely indulging in the oppression of mankind, and depriving human beings of their share of the justice and luminosity that is contained in God's religion. This is in contrast to the wars waged by the conquerors known to us from history, of whom it certainly cannot be said that they were fighting for the sake of justice, equal human rights and happiness for the whole of mankind!

If a people sought to defend its life and dignity and refused to accept humiliation, did not these world-conquering warriors become infuriated and order massacres and plundering to take place? Did Muhammad, upon whom be peace and blessings, have an aim similar to theirs? Did he engage in bloodshed to satisfy his own whims so that men would bow reverentially before his splendor and might and he might seize their property for his own use? Did not their conquests augment their arrogance and self-worship, and did they not use the booty of war to enhance the opulence of their rule? However ignorant and unjust a person might be, no one can attribute any of this to the Prophet of Islam.

The war waged by Muhammad, upon whom be peace and blessings, was a war of monotheism against polytheism. It was a struggle of light against darkness, and represented the last resort for the destruction of misguidance and the diffusion of virtue and justice. He was a reformer devoted to advancing the true life of the human being and he progressed unceasingly toward that lofty goal.

When the Prophet first proclaimed his mission, all the Arab tribes were prepared to submit to his rule and assign him all kinds of privilege, but he decisively rejected their proposals. He wished to unite the masses of mankind beneath the banner of virtue and Divine unity, to establish the government of reason and piety, and to guide mankind on the path to eternal felicity.

Today, after the passage of more than fourteen centuries, the triumph of the Prophet is fully apparent. The book that he brought, which includes within it the essence of all heavenly scriptures, guarantees the happiness of mankind, and the noble name of this lofty personage is reverentially mentioned by millions of human beings. His name resounds from all the minarets in the world with a great spiritual splendor, and it will always continue to do so, morning and evening, in accordance with a Divine promise, penetrating the souls of men and illumining their hearts. For God said in the Quran: *"We have elevated and borne on high your goodly name."* (94:4)

Lesson Twelve
Let Us Know the Quran Better

The means for establishing the messengerhood of the Prophet of Islam are those we have already expounded. The conditions and clear signs which must exist in every bearer of a heavenly message must be shown to exist also in the Prophet of Islam.

Prophethood and messengerhood are closely and inseparably linked to the miracle that proves the relationship of the claimant to prophethood with the supra-natural realm; the miracle is the clearest and most objective evidence that disarms those who would illogically deny prophethood, for it demonstrates that the claim of the Prophet is founded on a reality.

All the Prophets had but a single aim in fulfilling their Divine missions; their teachings are all of a similar type, notwithstanding the peculiarities of the mission of each, and the truths they expounded concerning the supra-natural realm differ only with respect to the degree of detail. It is true that there are differences with regard to acts of worship and social dealings; a common principle is implemented in differing ways that take into consideration the specific characteristics of each age and represent an evolutionary process.

It appears that one of the reasons for the variation in miracle, is that in the times of earlier Prophets, people were inclined to believe only on the basis of material observations of visible objects that lacked any spiritual content. The fetters imposed on human thought by the seers and sages of those times caused people's attention to be limited to a particular realm, which, in turn, was the most significant factor in separating them from God and causing their minds to stagnate. The destruction of such a limited mode of thought was therefore of necessity a principal aim of the Prophets.

The Prophets were entrusted by God with the duty of attacking this source of error by confronting the seers and soothsayers with deeds of a type similar to that which they performed, but enjoying a special advantage that placed them beyond the reach of all competition. By the power of the miracle they negated and destroyed that particular cause of the human beings' separation from God—the concentration of their attention on the dazzling acts performed by the soothsayers of the age which enslaved their spirits. By demonstrating their own miracles and setting forth the realistic principles of Divine religion, they opened the doors of guidance, growth, and development toward perfection, and linked all dimensions of human life and activity to God. All of this survives from the real nature of the miracle.

The Prophet of Islam began conveying his heavenly message in the midst of a society where people's minds revolved exclusively around eloquent speech and the composition of beautiful and attractive poetry and literary excellence. Precisely this concentration on a field of activity that cannot be counted among the basic and vital concerns of the human being was an important factor in prolonging the stagnation of thought and lack of attention to the source of all existence.

Under these conditions, God equipped His Prophet with a weapon, the Quran, that apparently belonged to the same category as the literary works of the age but possessed unique and astonishing characteristics that were beyond the capacity of the human being to reproduce.

The Quran's sweetness of speech, the attraction exerted by the verses of God's book, filled the hearts of the Arabs with new feeling and perception. Their deep attention was drawn to this Divine trust that had come to them, this inimitable work. Fully versed as they were in the arts and subtleties of rhetoric, they realized that the extraordinary eloquence of the Quran was beyond the power of man to produce. It was impossible for someone to hear the Quran and understand its meaning without being profoundly affected by its power to attract. From the beginning of revelation, the Quran was, then, the most important factor in bringing the human being to God's religion.

Moreover, if the Prophet of Islam had performed some miracle other than the Quran, it would have had no meaning for that people, given their mental structure. The path would have been open for all kinds of doubt and hesitation. But the Arabs of that age who were addressed by the Quran could never have any doubts about its extraordinary eloquence, for they were well aware of all the mysteries of rhetoric and had living among them masters of language and literary composition.

At the same time, since the Quran is intended to be an eternal miracle, revealed to make science and learning blossom among human beings, it is also a scientific miracle. It has expounded, in the most eloquent fashion, truths of a metaphysical nature together with everything that touches, however slightly, on the happiness of wretchedness of the human being. Although those who are not acquainted with the Arabic language cannot fully appreciate its miraculousness, they can perceive the miraculous nature of the meanings and truths it contains.

The limitation in time of the miracles performed by the earlier Prophets was an indication of the impermanence of their religions and the laws that they brought. By contrast, the miracle attesting to the prophethood fo the Prophet of Islam cannot be temporally limited, because his message is universal and represents the culmination of all preceding religions; his prophethood requires an eternal miracle, a brilliant and eloquent proof of its immortality.

A permanent message must display to mankind a permanent and everlasting miracle, one which advances with time, so that just as it offered convincing proof to people of the past, it may do the same to people of the future. A short-lived miracle that is imperceptible to later generations cannot be a source of reference or judgment for the future.

For this reason, the Quran is presented as a permanent and everlasting miracle, the final manifestation of God's revelation. The Quran itself says: *"The true and well-formulated message of your Lord has now been completed, and none is able to change it."* (6:115)

From the very first day when he presented his religion as a universal school of thought, the influence of which was not to be contained by geographical or ethnic boundaries, the Prophet of Islam displayed this proof of his messengerhood to the whole of mankind, as a living proof that his mission and the revolutionary movement he inaugurated represented the final chapter in the history of prophetic missions and movements.

The Quran does not represent an ideological weapon for

temporary use in moving from an inferior social system to a superior one at a given stage in history; it represents the permanent ideology of the human being living in the social and intellectual order of Islam.

The miracle accompanying the mission of the beloved Prophet of Islam brings to an end all the previous messages, limited as they were to a certain time. In its unique style, the Quran provides the human being with all necessary guidance by means of either recalling the circumstances leading to the revelation of various verses or of recounting of historical narratives or of describing the events that took place during the life of the Prophet, or by means of various similes and comparisons that touch on the different concerns of human life and guide the human being in the direction of higher degrees. By analyzing the stories and events contained in the Quran, which include also a distinctively Quranic mode of judgment, it is possible to deduce certain general principles.

Although the gradual and orderly descent of the Quranic revelation was regarded as a defect by superficial and ignorant people, it should, in fact, be recognized as a principal factor in the triumph of the Prophet's message, given the conditions of the age and the events with which he was confronted.

Just as chronic diseases require long-term treatment, a continuous struggle against the factors that constantly prevent the human being from perceiving the truths of existence and stand in the way of his growth and development must be grounded on a firm ideational basis and a comprehensive social organization. Only then will it be able to implement its goals over a period of time and guide human beings to its ultimate purpose—their liberation from self-alienation.

Solutions whose efficacy does not transcend events limited in time and space will be unable to solve the problems of the human being. Islam represents the only system which is able to answer those problems because of the attention it pays to all phenomena.

For Muslims, the miraculousness of the Quran is a matter of religious belief; for scholars and researchers, it is a matter of scientific belief. The Quran possesses a remarkable comprehensiveness and richness, with respect to its worldview and scientific content, and its ability to guide the individual and society. There are still many matters contained in the Quran that call for investigation and await discovery by further research.

The Extraordinary Richness of the Quran

The Quran represents the principal source of all researches concerning the Islamic school of thought. Moreover, in every age and every part of the world, it can serve as the basis for a developed and free society which enables all the hidden capacities and potentials of the human being to blossom in all their dimensions; it lays down a path to the ideal society and the government of God.

More than fourteen centuries have passed since the revelation of the Quran. Throughout this period, mankind has undergone numerous changes, and passing through repeated stages of development and growth, it has attained a more comprehensive awareness of the mysteries of creation. Nonetheless, the Quran has at all times retained its proud and dignified presence on the stage of human history.

When this miracle first came into existence, at a time when the foundations of human thought had not fully developed, it served to prove categorically the messengerhood of the Prophet of Islam. In the present age, as the human being discovers in the treasure house of the Quran, more and more remarkable indications, commensurate with his own growth in perception, knowledge and civilization, the Quran still stands as a permanent historical miracle and a living universal proof for the veracity of the Seal of the Prophets. The increase in the volume of human knowledge and the opening up of new horizons of thought have given us the chance to benefit more fully from the Quran than past generations.

If the Quran had been able to establish itself only during a certain segment of time and in a limited spatial environment, it would not have been able thus miraculously to advance together with time. The reason for the eternal vitality and authenticity of the Quran is that it has always been a source for spiritual guidance and command in the face of the changing events of time.

History bears witness that the emergence of the Seal of the Prophets and his mode of activity within society marked the beginning of a new stage in human thought and ratiocination and in the development and expansion of the will and independence of the human being. For in his growth to maturity, the human being now advanced in his investigations from the stage of mere observation to that of thought; an exact and profound examination of phenomena took the place of simplistic assumption.   All this is indicated by the fact that the human beings' acceptance of true faith was no longer on the basis of miracles involving supranatural or extraordinary phenomena, as was the case with the mission of previous Prophets.

Human beings turning to faith on the basis of knowledge and thought—something to which the Quran repeatedly invites human beings—represents in itself the miracle wrought by the heavenly message of Islam. Reliance on sensory miracles would not have been compatible with the nature of the final Divine message and its aim of liberating the human being and fostering the growth of his intellect. God, therefore, prepared the human being in the course of many thousands of years to receive the final guidance.

Our investigations of the Quran can be of value only when we empty our minds of all pre-existing notions and attitudes, because fanatical convictions concerning the contents of the Quran will yield nothing but mental stagnation and immobility. This is a pitfall that every alert and fair-minded researcher must seek to avoid.

It is an undeniable reality that the Quran is too elevated a book to be the product of ideas held by a group of scholars. It is even more impossible for it to have been produced by a single individual or to have been borrowed by him from other sources, particularly an individual who was unlettered, had not even studied, and had grown up in the degenerate environment of the Arabian peninsula at that time, an environment which was totally alien to science and philosophy.

When we consider the system and program of action proposed by the Quran for the uplift of the human being and compare it with the laws and systems of the past, we realize that it borrowed nothing from them and bore no resemblance to them. It represents an entirely new phenomenon, original and unprecedented in its fundamental nature, and among its lofty aims are the transformation of human societies and their restructuring on the basis of justice, equality, and freedom for the oppressed and deprived masses.

The Quran speaks in detail of the history of earlier Prophets and their communities, referring constantly to the events that occurred during their careers. When we encounter the narratives contained in the Quran, the events that it relates, we are brought into direct contact with reality, in an unparalleled fashion. Every reference they contain, direct and indirect, acquaints us with the very substance of truth. It is, then, totally impossible that the narratives of the Quran should have been borrowed from the Torah or the Gospels. The Quran always presents the stories of the Prophets in a positive framework by changing and modifying them so as to purge them of unworthy excesses and elements contrary to pure monotheism, reason, and sound religious thinking. A copying would have resulted in mere imitation, and would have been entirely negative.

Dr. Murice Bucaille, the French scholar, expresses himself as follows on this point. "In the West, Jews, Christians and Atheists are unanimous in stating (without a scrap of evidence, however) that Muhammad wrote the Quran or had it written as an imitation of the Bible. It is claimed that stories of religious history in the Quran resume Biblical stories. This attitude is as thoughtless as saying that Jesus Himself duped His contemporaries by drawing inspiration from the Old Testament during His preachings: the whole of Matthew's Gospel is based on this continuation of the Old Testament.... What expert in exegesis would dream of depriving Jesus of his status as God's envoy for this reason?

"The existence of such an enormous difference between the Biblical description and the data in the Quran concerning the Creation is worth underlining once again on account of the totally gratuitous accusations leveled against Muhammad since the beginnings of Islam to the effect that he copied the Biblical descriptions. As far as the Creation is concerned, this accusation is totally unfounded. *How could a man living fourteen hundred years ago have made corrections to the existing description to such an extent that he eliminated scientifically inaccurate material and, on his own initiative, made statements that science has been able to verify only in the present day? This hypothesis is completely untenable. The description of the Creation given in the Quran is quite different from the one in the Bible.*"[29]

Taking these factors into consideration, no truth-loving individual can conceive of an origin other than Divine revelation for the Quran which is not only a book, but also a proof of messengerhood and a manifestation of the miraculousness that supported the

Prophet.

The Quran thus came to be the profound, brilliant and eternal miracle of God's Messenger enabling the teachings and laws of Islam to retain their validity through time. The Divine commands and instructions were made manifest in phrases and sentences that were marked by miraculousness, thus implementing God's will for the preservation of religion when faced with the assaults of rancorous enemies and for the frustration of their conspiracies.

Through the permanence and stability of the mould in which God's Commands are uniquely set, these enemies who would reach out against them in order to change and distort them are permanently prevented from attaining their goal; the eternal teachings and laws of God will last throughout time, immune from change or distortion.

Another aspect of the miraculousness of the Quran which has had a great effect is the revolutionary transformation it brought about in human civilization. A matter calling for serious attention in the study of Islam is the fact that it received no assistance from factors external to itself when it began to create the nucleus of a universal society out of a scattered and disunited people that lacked all science and free thought and did not even seek to unify its constituent tribes; and when it began, moreover, to found a uniquely, vast and spiritual civilization. All the factors for changing the world, for putting forward an international law with the slogan of unity among races, peoples, and social classes, for creating a movement for the liberation of thought and the ennobling of knowledge, were derived from the very text of the Quran, from the culture that emerged from the Quran and from the Islamic order. Islam never relied on a government or a power situated outside the society it had itself brought into being.

Even the aggressors who attacked the Islamic lands and triumphed over the Muslims, thanks to their military superiority, lost their dominance in the end when they were confronted with the spiritual power of Islam, and they adopted the religion of the people they had conquered. This history of nations does not record any other example of a victorious aggressor adopting the religion of the people it had defeated.

Lesson Thirteen
The Demand of the Quran
for a Direct Confrontation

The Noble Quran was revealed in the Arabic language, one of the richest languages in the world from the point of view of firmness of structure and abundance of vocabulary. It descended like a flash of lightning in the darkness of the Age of Ignorance, and in the manner in which it conveyed various types of subject matter in the most concise of sentences it had nothing in common with the conventional language of the Arabs.

At the time that the Quran was revealed, the literary talent and eloquence of the Arabs was at its peak. Works created by poets and orators commanded the attention and admiration of everyone, and literature constituted the only art cultivated by the Arab elite.

The Quran, which constituted the documentary proof of the messengerhood of the Prophet of Islam and the raw materials of which its constituent letters and words was revealed over a period of twenty-three years in accordance with the particular needs that emerged over time. Thus it guided the Prophet and his companions step by step toward their exalted goals.

The words and expressions of the Quran are harmonious and its words are set together pleasingly and with the utmost beauty, and in complete accord with the subtle meanings they express. This unique combination of wording and meaning is a special feature of the Quran and another aspect of its miraculousness.

With the revelation of the Quran, the Arabs made the acquaintance of a a fresh and new form of speech which was neither prose nor poetry, but the melody of which was more beautiful and attractive than that of poetry and the discourse of which was more eloquent and effective than that of prose. Whoever heard it was

drawn toward it and transformed by it. It was utterly different
from all forms of human speech by virtue of the superiority of its
concepts, the eloquence of its style and outward form, and its
exposition of meanings in the most concise way.

The firm laws and clear logic of the Quran showed human
beings the way to correct religion and living, and inspired them
with the determination to create an epic unparalleled in history.
The Quran destroyed utterly the superstitions that the oppressors
and their helpers had elaborated throughout history.

The Quran established a mode of thought leading to the truth,
which is identified as thought that eschews all obstinacy, caprice
and fanaticism. From the very first day that the Prophet began
preaching his message of monotheism, he summoned people also
to a realistic vision of the world. When inviting them to faith, he
addressed their wisdom and intelligence and called on them to use
their eyes and their ears to perceive the truth. He unshackled them
from custom and usage, from obstinately clinging to ancient heri-
tages, and strove to convince them that they should not perversely
insist on retaining the beliefs and loyalties that had been born of
polytheism. Although these efforts earned him bitter harassment,
he was not dismayed, and he did not give up before fulfilling the
role that the Creator had given him in improving men's lives.

Many of the polytheists did not permit themselves to listen to
the Quran for they were well aware of its remarkable effect and
afraid that its profound and astonishing influence might conquer
their hearts as well, drawing them ineluctably towards it.

Ibn Hisham writes in his life of the Prophet: "So strong was the
heartfelt desire of the people to hear the Quran that even some of
the unbelievers of the Quraysh would stealthily go near the Prophet's
house at night, remaining there until dawn, in order to listen
throughout the night to the pleasing melody of the Quran as recited
by the Messenger of God. This happened many times."[30]

When the revelation of the Quran began, the Most Noble
Messenger clearly proclaimed the Quran to be the Word of God,
and said it was impossible for any human being to duplicate it; if
anyone disagreed, he ought to make an attempt to copy it, and
should feel free to seek help from any source in doing so. None was
able to take up this challenge and produce even a short surah
similar to the Quran.

Still more remarkable is the fact that the utterances of the Prophet, whose tongue would recite the Quran, bore no resemblance whatsoever to the Quran. This is in itself a convincing proof that the Quran originated from a source other than the mind of the Prophet.

The Quran Modifies the Conditions of its Challenge

The Quran issued a challenge not only to the contemporaries of the Prophet but also to men in all ages. In order to demonstrate the incapacity and impotence of people to imitate it, it issued the following universal proclamation: *"Were all of mankind to come together and wish to produce the like of the Quran, they would never succeed, however much they aided each other."* (17:88)

It then modifies the challenge and reduces its scope by saying: *"Do people imagine that this Quran is not from Us, and that you, Oh Prophet, are falsely attributing it to Us? Tell them that if they are speaking truly they should produce ten surahs resembling the Quran, and that they are free to call on the aid of anyone but God in so doing."* (11:13)

Then, at a third stage, the scope of the challenge is reduced still further: the deniers are called on to produce only a single *surah* resembling the Quran: *"Oh people, if you doubt the heavenly origin of this Book which We have sent down to Our servant, the Prophet, produce one surah like it."* (2:23)

Since we know that some of the shorter *surahs* consist only of a few brief sentences, this final challenge constituted a definitive proof of the human being's inability to imitate the Quran.

It is remarkable that the Prophet who thus challenged the Arabs to a kind of literary contest, despite all their literary resources, was someone who had never in the course of the forty years of his life participated in any of their literary competitions or acquired any superiority in eloquence over this own people.

Let us not forget that this challenge was issued to a people whose leaders were threatened by the devastating attacks of the Quran—their lives, their property, their ancient customs, their ancestors, their whole social position. If it had been at all possible for the Arabs to respond to the challenge of the Quran, they would have taken it up immediately, with the unstinting aid of the masters of eloquence that were by no means rare in that age. Thus they would have invalidated the proofs of the Quran and won an everlasting victory.

Furthermore, as a matter of general principle, if one consistently follows and studies the style of a certain form of speech, he will ultimately be able to imitate it. But the Quran forms an exception to this rule: however much one tries to practice the use of the Quranic style, he will never be able to create something resembling the Quran. This reveals to us a significant truth: mere learning and study can never give us the capability to imitate the Quran. History has not a single instance to show in which this particular aspect of the miraculousness of the Quran has been negated; it cannot point to a single book comparable to the Quran. Even among the speeches and sayings of the Prophet, nothing can be found which resembles the Quran from the point of view of style and eloquence.

If the forces opposing Islam, with all of their skilled rhetoricians, had been able to create works capable of competing with the Quran, there would have been no need for them to endure losses and casualties by going to war, to suffer hardship and expend material resources. They could have won an easy victory by means of propaganda, a kind of cold war, and put paid to the rise of Islam within itself, its place of origin.

They called into play all their resources in an effort to meet the challenge of the Quran, but all their efforts came to naught. They were unable to point even to a single error or defect in the Quran and were obliged to admit that its words were situated on a higher plane than the thought and speech of the human being.

The verses of the Quran penetrated the depths of human beings' hearts with such unprecedented swiftness that all people of sound mind and heroic disposition eagerly embraced its message. By contrast, the devotees of ignorance and mental stagnation, people who assigned little value to wisdom and thought, and whose lives were spent in the swamp of neglect and lack of awareness, were the principal element in opposing Islam and urging others to do so. In order to conceal from people's view the miraculous nature of the Quran, they attributed the Quran to the workings of magic, seeking thus to explain the extraordinary attraction exerted by its verses and its unique influence.

Sometimes they would also subject the converts to Islam to harassment and a hail of contempt and ridicule, or through force and coercion they would attempt to prevent the people from thinking freely. Their whole method of struggle against Islam was, in fact, childish, and it betrayed their weakness and utter helplessness.

For example, they instructed a group of people to go and make a noise, to whistle and clap their hands, while the Prophet was reciting the verses of the Quran, so that the people would not fall under the influence of its eloquence and power to attract.

The methods followed by the leaders of Quraysh and their insistence on preventing the message of the Quran from reaching the ears of the people showed that a deadly serious struggle between truth and falsehood was not indeed underway.

The Quran itself unmasks the methods they followed and the negative role that they played: *"The polytheists said: 'Do not listen to the verses of the Quran, and make a noise while they are being recited; perhaps you will thus triumph.' "* (41:26)

But this attempt forcibly to sever the connection between people's minds and the Quran did not last long. As soon as the shackles of coercion and fear were loosened from the minds of people, even some of the leaders of the polytheists who were firmly attached to the rites and customs of the Age of Ignorance would conceal themselves behind the coverings of the Ka'bah not far from where the Prophet was sitting, in order to listen to him reciting the verses of the Quran in prayer. This shows how deeply the image the Quran had traced of itself was able to penetrate deep into the souls of the people, so that the polytheists were ultimately unable to accomplish anything effective against the message of the Quran, although it represented a call to battle fatal to their interests.

This impotence on the part of the enemies of Islam belongs to the dawn of Islam: the masters of eloquence were unable to imitate or compete with the Quran.

Now that we are in the fifteenth century since the Quran first laid down its challenge, a time when the progress of learning has opened up new horizons of thought in front of us, we can appreciate the Divine origin of the Quran and its infinite values by reference to other matters, quite apart from the unique and inimitable structure and eloquence of the Quran. We can perceive the Quran to be an everlasting miracle, because the position of revelation vis-a-vis its deniers remains firmly the same, and the challenge of the Quran still resounds to all of mankind: *"If you doubt the heavenly origin of this book, produce one surah like it."* (2:23)

Can the person of today take up the challenge of the Quran and produce a *surah* like it, thereby conquering the stronghold of Islam and invalidating the claims of its Prophet?

Both in past and present times, there have been obstinate and impudent enemies of Islam among the experts on Arabic language and literature. If it had been possible for them to meet the challenge of the Quran, that eternal miracle of harmony and symmetry, and produce a single *surah* like it, they would certainly have devoted themselves fully to such a destructive undertaking.

Islam has proposed,then, a very simple challenge to those who oppose it.   Why then do the deniers of prophethood choose roundabout ways, avoiding this direct method of confronting and defeating Islam?   Is it not because the door is firmly closed on meeting the challenge posed by the Quran?

Gibb, a certain Christian scholar, says: "Even if we attempt to reorder the words of the Quran, we will not be able to put them in a new and meaningful order; we must replace them exactly where they were before."

Despite the passage of time, historical documents and evidence still provide such a clear picture of the Prophet of Islam and his characteristics that all historians are unanimous that the Prophet was an unlettered man who had never known books or teachers and never learned how to write. The Quran itself addressed him as follows, proclaiming his characteristics to the members of Meccan society who were acquainted with all the stages of his life: *"Before this, you did not read any book, nor did you write anything with your hands."* (29:48) The Divine nature of the Prophet's message is thus demonstrated.

Is it at all possible that someone should proclaim to the members of his own society, in utter contradiction of the truth, that he is unlettered and has never studied, without anyone voicing an objection?   The dark cultural environment of that day was, in any event, a stranger to scholars and teachers; nothing existed that the Prophet might have studied. Those people who knew how to read and write were few and far between and none of the historians records a single instance of the Prophet having read a single line or written a single word before the beginning of his prophetic mission.

How remarkable it is that such a man who had never studied became the standard-bearer of a movement calling for science and free thought! With the beginning of his messengerhood and his entry on the stage of human history, mankind entered a new stage of progress. With the suddenness of a flash of lightening, he introduced his people to the world of learning and writing and laid the foundations of a movement that transformed the degenerate society of Arabia into the nucleus of a great world civilization. A few centuries later, that civilization could boast of the most splendid scientific accomplishments and the greatest scholars and researchers.

A consideration of these facts concerning the phenomenon of Islam, particularly as they are judged by non-Muslim scholars, helps us to understand better the profoundly miraculous nature of the Quran. The author of *Muhammad, the Prophet Who Must Be Examined Anew*, writes as follows: "Although he was unlettered, the very first verses that were revealed to him contain mention of the pen and of knowledge, of learning and teaching. There is no other religion that places such emphasis, in its very origin, on knowledge and learning.

"If Muhammad had been a scholar, the revelation of the Quran in the cave of Hira would not have been surprising, for a scholar knows well the value of learning. But he was unlettered and had never studied with any teacher. I congratulate the Muslims that the acquisition of knowledge was so highly valued at the very inception of their religion."[31]

Laura Vaccia Vaglieri, professor at the University of Naples, has the following to say: "The heavenly book of Islam is miraculous and inimitable. Its style is totally unprecedented in Arabic literature, and its peculiar impact on the spirit of the human being derives from its special and superior characteristics. How is it possible that such a book should be the work of Muhammad, an Arab who had never studied?

"We find in this book a treasury of knowledge beyond the capacity of the greatest philosophers and statesmen, and for this reason it is also impossible to regard the Quran as the work of an educated person."

Smith writes in his book, *Muhammad and Islam*: "I boldly assert that one day the loftiest of human philosophers and the most veracious principles of Christianity will confess and bear witness that the Quran is the Word of God and that Muhammad is the Messenger of God. An unlettered and unlearned Prophet was chosen by God to bring the Quran to mankind, a book that has in the course of history produced thousands of other books and treatises, brought libraries into being and filled them with books, and placed before mankind laws and philosophies and educational, intellectual and ideological systems.

"He arose in an environment where there was no trace of learning and civilization. In the whole of Medina, there were only eleven people who knew how to read and write, and in all the branches of the Quraysh, in Mecca and its environs, not more than seventeen people were literate.

"The teachings of the Quran, which mentions knowledge and the pen in its opening verses, brought about a tremendous transformation. Islam proclaimed study to be a religious duty, and made the black ink of the scribe and the scholar to be superior to the red blood of the martyr.

"Thanks to the teachings of the Quran and its emphasis on the cultivation of knowledge, countless scholars made their appearance and wrote innumerable books. Different scientific disciplines were derived from the Quran and spread across the world by Muslim thinkers. The world was illumined with the light of the Quran and the culture of Islam."

Lesson Fourteen
The Relationship of the Quran to Modern Science: Part I

The Quran deserves to be evaluated from different points of view. One topic for examination is the artistic and verbal beauty of the Quran and its style which is neither poetry nor prose. It does not have the characteristics of poetry, which may be thought as giving free flight to the imagination and indulging in poetic exaggeration, and equally it does not exemplify conventional prose, for it is imbued with a distinctive rhythm and melody that are the means for it to exert a powerful and unique spiritual attraction on all who make its acquaintance.

Then the intellectual and scientific content of the Quran also calls for examination. It is true that it is not the aim of the Noble Quran to uncover and expound scientific phenomena, to set forth all the natural motions and events that occur within the system of being in accordance with a specific set of laws, or to explain the properties and mode of operation of nature.

We should not expect the Quran to discuss, in an organized manner, the various branches of science and to analyze the topics connected with each of those branches, or to solve the various problems that are encountered in different fields of research. The ability to experiment and to conduct scientific research has been made inherent in the human being's nature, and he can obtain the knowledge and the arts he needs in his life by means of thought and reflection. He makes valuable advances through his unceasing efforts to gain control over the forces of nature. Concerns such as these are alien to a book of moral edification.

The aim pursued by the Quran is the training of the human being as a being conscious of his duties; it reinforces and accelerates his spiritual ascension, together with all of his qualities, toward a state of true loftiness and the dignity of which the human being is worthy. The emergence of such a being requires a comprehensive reform of the human being, involving various changes such as the negation of false values and meaningless criteria deriving from the Age of Ignorance and the creation and fostering of a creative energetic spirit within him. The Quran can thus be said to melt the spirits of human beings and pour them into a new mould, where they acquire a different, richer and more valuable form.

Although this may be said to be the principal aim of the Quran, it summons the human being insistently, at the very same time, to reflect and to ponder, and to acquire a realistic view of the world; it guides him on to the path of thought, of teaching and learning.

In the very first verses of the Quran to be revealed, we encounter praise and ennobling of the pen, of the acquisition of knowledge and of the study of nature as one of the principal sources of cognition; a profound awareness of nature may lead to the boundaries of the supranatural realm. Through the inspiration given by the Quran and as a result of the scientific movement launched by Islam, a vital and active people blossomed into maturity, uniquely gifted with knowledge and virtue. The viewpoint of Islam on science represented a major development that prepared the way for subsequent developments.

Iqbal, the well-known Indo-Muslim thinker, says: "The birth of Islam, as I hope to be able presently to prove to your satisfaction, is the birth of inductive intellect...The constant appeal to reason and experience in the Quran, and the emphasis that it lays on Nature and History as sources of human knowledge, are all different aspects of the same idea of finality.

"Inner experience is only one source of human knowledge. According to the Quran, there are two other sources of knowledge—Nature and History; and it is in tapping these sources of knowledge that the spirit of Islam is seen at its best."[32]

All forms of scientific endeavor are necessarily based on respect for the intellect and for the development of the human being and on freedom of thought from all kinds of fetters. The principal advances and developments in the natural sciences are all due to these premises.

The contemporary human being is heir to the knowledge and

the researches of millions of thinkers and scholars who in their investigations discovered the foundations of the various sciences, and who gained access to some of the mysteries of being by means of their intellectual originality and creativity and their untiring efforts.

In the age when the Quran was revealed—an age known as the Age of Ignorance—creative and innovative thought, marked by the comprehensive spirit of science, was non-existent, and no one was able to discern the mysteries of the vast, unknown universe.

When expounding the mysteries of creation, the Quran is clear and explicit whenever clarity and explicitness are desirable. In cases where the perception of complex truths was difficult for the people of that age, the Quran contents itself with making allusions, so that in the course of time as the intellects and knowledge of human beings developed and the mysteries of nature came more clearly to the fore, these matters would become more easily comprehensible.

In expounding the contents of the Quran, Muslim scholars have continually put forward different views, as a result both of their own researches, investigations and reflections, and of the vast spiritual richness of the Quran. Given this spiritual richness, it is inconceivable that such a great and infinite source of truth could have been produced by the talent and intellectual genius of the human being.

If something takes place by way of natural causation, it should be possible for people living either at the time of its first occurrence or in a later age to produce something similar. But if a phenomenon takes place outside the natural course of things, so that natural laws and criteria are suspended, people will be unable at all times to attempt its replication.

In the case of the Quran, we see that all conventional criteria and principles were violated; the entirety of the book represents a transcendence of all norms.

We have said that the Quran refers allusively to scientific truths, almost as secondary matters serving as a preliminary to the attainment of a greater and more glorious goal. We cannot, therefore, regard it as a technical work of specialization that discusses matters only from the viewpoint of science.

The Quran refers to certain aspects of the life of the human being, the earth, the heavens and the plants, but it would be entirely wrong to imagine that it does so with the intention of elucidating the natural sciences or resolving dubious points connected with them. The purpose of the Quran is rather to expound truths that are relevant to the spiritual life of the human being and the exaltation of his being and conducive to his attaining a life of true happiness.

Furthermore, when expounding scientific truths which might be couched in a different terminology in every age, the Quran does not make use of technical terms. For although scientific truths and the laws governing all phenomena enjoy stability and immutability, and although they have always existed and always will exist, it is possible that scientific terminology might change from one age to the next and appear in a totally different form from before.

Discussions in the Quran concerning the world of creation relate to a series of truths and principles that are not situated in the sensory realm. The human being can grasp these matters only by recourse to particular scientific instruments.

Dr. Bucaille, the French scientist, writes as follows: "A crucial fact is that the Quran, while inviting us to cultivate science, itself contains many observations on natural phenomena and includes explanatory details which are seen to be in total agreement with modern scientific data. There is no equal to this in the Judeo-Christian Revelation.

"These scientific considerations, which are very specific to the Quran, greatly surprised me at first. Up until then, I had not thought it possible for one to find so many statements in a text compiled more than thirteen centuries ago referring to extremely diverse subjects and all of them totally in keeping with modern scientific knowledge...A thorough linguistic knowledge is not in itself sufficient to understand these verses from the Quran. What is needed along with this is a highly diversified knowledge of science. A study such as the present one embraces many disciplines and is in that sense encyclopedic. As the questions raised are discussed, the variety of scientific knowledge essential to the understanding of certain verses of the Quran will become clear.

"The Quran does not aim at explaining certain laws governing the Universe, however; it has an absolutely basic religious objective. The descriptions of Divine Omnipotence are what principally incite the human being to reflect on the works of Creation. They are accompanied by references to facts accessible to human observation or to laws defined by God who presides over the organization of the universe both in the sciences of nature.

"One part of these assertions is easily understood, but the meaning of the other can only be grasped if one has the essential scientific knowledge it requires...

"The hypothesis advanced by those who see Muhammad as the author of the Quran is quite untenable. How could a man, from being illiterate, become the most important author, in terms of literary merit, in the whole of Arabic literature? How could he then pronounce truths of a scientific nature that no other human being could possibly have developed at the time, and all this without once making the slightest error in his pronouncements on the subject?

"The ideas in this study are developed from a purely scientific point of view. They lead to the conclusion that it is inconceivable for a human being living in the seventh century A.D. to have made statements in the Quran on a great variety of subjects that do not belong to his period and for them to be in keeping with what was to be known only centuries later. For me, there can be no human explanation to the Quran." [33]

Let us briefly examine a few examples of this kind of topic. One, the best-known theory concerning the emergence of the solar system is the hypothesis of Laplace, some of whose views were later refuted by certain scientists as a result of further research.

Although there are other views concerning the factors that caused the emergence of the solar system, all scientific circles in the world today are agreed that the planets were originally composed of a mass of sodium gas: first the heavens and the earth were joined together as a single entity and then they separated from each other.

Centuries ago, the Quran alluded to this scientific theory. It says, when describing the creation of the heavens: *"Then God turned to the creation of the heavens (the planets), when they were but a smoky substance."* (41:11) *"Do the unbelievers not see that the heavens and the earth were joined together before We separated them, and that We brought all living things into existence from water? Why do they still not believe in God?"* (21:30)

The well-known scientist Gamof says: "As we know, the sun came into being out of cumulative gases, and the sun then emitted a series of gases from itself that came into being after the separation from it of the planets. How did this burning mass of planetary matter come into being and what forces were involved in its origination? Who assembled the materials needed for their construction?

"These are questions which confront us with respect to the moon as well as every other planet in the solar system; they form the basis of all cosmological theories and are riddles that have preoccupied astronomers for centuries."[34]

James, an English scientist, writes: "Millions of centuries ago, a planet was passing in the vicinity of the sun and created an awesome tidal effect, so that matter separated from the sun in the shape of a long cigarette. Then this matter was divided: the weightier portion of the cigarette became the great planets, and the lighter portions brought the lesser planets into being."[35]

The words used by the Quran in the verse quoted above, attributing the origin of the heavens to smoke (=gas), indicates the profundity with which this Divine book treats matters. All scientists are of the opinion that sodium is a gas mixed with ferrous materials, and the word smoke/gas may be taken to include both gas and iron. The word 'smoke' is, then, the most scientific expression that might be employed in the context.

Thus the Quran unveils one of the great mysteries of nature: the separation of the planets from a huge object and then their separation from each other. Since at the time of the revelation of the Quran, the general level of knowledge and science was extremely low, does this not constitute a proof of the heavenly nature of the Quran?

Does not the exposition of these matters by the Quran, in a manner conforming to quite recent discoveries made by astronomers, prove that the voice speaking in the Quran belongs to one who is acquainted with all the mysteries and truths of existence?

Dr. Bucaille makes the following open admission: "At the earliest time it can provide us with, modern science has every reason to maintain that the Universe was formed of a gaseous mass principally composed of hydrogen and a certain amount of helium that was slowly rotating. This nebula subsequently split up into multiple fragments with very large dimensions and masses, so large indeed, that specialists in astrophysics are able to estimate their mass from 1 to 100 billion times the present mass of the Sun (the latter represents a mass that is over 300,000 times that of the Earth). These figures give an idea of the large size of the fragments of primary gaseous mass that were to give birth to the galaxies.

"It must be noted, however, that the formation of the heavenly bodies and the Earth, as explained in verses 9 to 12, surah 41....required two phases. If we take the Sun and its sub-product, the Earth as an example (the only one accessible to us), science informs us that their formation occurred by a process of condensation of the primary nebula and then their separation. This is exactly what the Quran expresses very clearly when it refers to the processes that produced a fusion and subsequent separation starting from a celestial 'smoke'. Hence there is complete correspondence between the facts of the Quran and the facts of science.

"Such statements in the Quran concerning the Creation, which appeared nearly fourteen centuries ago, obviously do not lend themselves to a human explanation."[36]

Two, one of the most subtle problems in science concerns the expansion of the universe, its tendency constantly to extend its boundaries. This was something completely unknown to the human being until the last century. This mystery is, however, mentioned by the Quran in the following terms, which again bear witness to its remarkable profundity when discussing such matters: *"We created the heavens with Our strength and power, and constantly expand them."* (51:47)

This verse speaks in categorical terms of the expansion of the universe, its constellations and galaxies, although not more than a century has passed since the discovery of the expansion of the universe.

The well-known scholar Baresht writes as follows: "Astronomers gradually became aware that certain regular motions were underway in the most distant galaxies that were barely visible to their telescopes. Those distant galaxies appear to be moving away both from the solar system and from each other.

"The regular flight of these galaxies, the closest of which is five hundred light-years away from us, is completely different from the placid motion of attraction exerted by bodies close to us. Those distant motions may have an effect on the curvature of the universe. The universe is not, then, in a state of immobility and balance; it is more like a soap bubble or a bellows in its constant expansion."[37]

Another scholar, John Pfeffer, writes as follows: "The universe is expanding. Wherever we look, we see the galaxies becoming more distant from each other; the distance between them is constantly growing. The most distant galaxies are becoming ever more removed from us, at the greatest conceivable speed. For example, while you have been reading this sentence, some of the galaxies will have become 250,000 miles farther removed from the earth.

"The parts of the universe are becoming farther removed from each other. It is as if a bullet had exploded in the air, the galaxies corresponding to the particles of the bullet as they hasten farther and farther apart. The theory of the big bang is based on precisely such a comparison.

"According to this theory, there was a time when all the matter in the universe was gathered together into a single dense mass. It was a substance suspended in space, with a volume hundreds of times greater than the sun, and resembled a bomb ready to explode. Then, about ten billion years ago, the explosion took place with a blinding flash, and the huge ball of matter became scattered in space. Its components are still being scattered forth in every direction, in a process of unceasing expansion—gases, rays, galaxies."[38]

The Glorious Quran draws people's attention to the splendor inherent in the ordering of the universe and the complexity of its creation, and it reminds them that the signs of the Creator's workmanship are so numerous in the universe that if the human being reflects aright he will inevitably come to believe in the eternal power of God, the source of all being. Then he will bow humbly before His magnificence.

We read in Surah al-Imran: "Certainly in the creation of the heavens and earth and in the alternation of night and day, there are clear signs for the intelligent, those who at all times make remembrance of God and constantly reflect on the creation of the heavens and the earth and say: 'Oh Creator! You have not created this expanse of splendor and magnificence in vain; You are pure and transcendent, so preserve us through Your favor from the torment of the fire.' "(3:190-91)

Lesson Fifteen
The Relationship of the
Quran to Modern Science: Part II

Three, the Quran describes as follows the factor that keeps each of the heavenly bodies on its appointed course: *"God it is Who raised up the heavenly bodies to invisible pillars and then took repose on the throne. He has subjected the sun and the moon to you, and each of them continues to rotate for a fixed time. Thus God regulates all the affairs of the universe and He explains in detail His signs, so that you may believe with certainty in the Day of Resurrection and the meeting with your Lord."* (13:2)

We know that before the time of Newton, that great scientific personality, no one was aware of the force of gravity. Although Newton made many discoveries in different branches of science, he is world-famous above all for the discovery of gravity. His achievement has been described as follows: "Newton proved that the falling of objects to earth, the rotation of the moon and Venus, the motions of the planets, and other instances of attraction are all subject to a single law, the law of universal gravity."[39]

One of the most difficult problems Newton encountered was how to prove that the gravitational force exerted by a globular body is the same as it would be if we were to regard the whole of the body as concentrated in its center. As long as this remained unproven, the theory of universal gravitation would represent a kind of inspiration, not based on precise calculations or mathematical proofs.

In the verse quoted above, the fixing of the heavenly bodies in space and their rotation in a fixed course are attributed to a factor designated as "invisible pillars." Are these unseen pillars, which prevent the planets from colliding with each other or falling, anything other than the mysterious and invisible force of universal gravity, a law to which the Creator of the universe has subjected all of the heavenly bodies?

Four, in conveying this scientific truth, the Quran has used an expression that is comprehensible for the men of all ages. The Eighth Imam, upon whom be peace, spoke as follows to one of his companions concerning this Quranic expression: "Did God not say in the Quran, *'without a pillar that you may see'*?"

The companion answered, "Yes," whereupon the Imam added "In that case there is a pillar but it cannot be seen."[40]

In the course of refuting the materialist view that the human being is destined to utter annihilation, the Quran describes the evolutionary movement of the universe saying, *"Do the deniers not look at the heavens above them and see how We have placed them on a firm foundation, adorned them with the stars and made them immune to all flaws? Were We tired by their first creation (so that We might experience difficulty in creating them anew)? They (the unbelievers) are themselves clothed every instant in a new garment of creation."* (50:6, 7, 15)

In other words, those who because of their shortsightedness and narrowness of vision imagined the world to be stagnant and stationary are in error, because they are themselves in a state of constant motion, together with the entire universe. The motion of the human being is connected to the general motion of the universe, and after death, too, his spiritual motion will continue, through the appearance of the Promised Day and the fulfillment of the Divine promise; his motion will never be cut short by death.

In expounding this precise scientific truth, the Quran does not restrict itself to the dry philosophical aspects of the matter. By entrusting the discussion of the matter to the Prophet, a person who had never studied, who had grown up in a spiritually dark environment with no philosophical tradition, the Quran simultaneously puts forward a truth that is of vital significance to the human being. That truth is the immortality of the spirit, the existence of resurrection and judgment, with all that that implies for the responsibilities of the human being while still alive.

The Quran also refers to the internal motion of the earth when it says: *"You look at the mountains and imagine them to be solid and stable. But they are engaged in inward motion and growth, just like the clouds. This inward motion if of God's creation and making: He has fashioned all things in a correct way, and He is well aware of your conduct and deeds."* (16:90)

This verse calls attention to the inward dynamic motion of mountains. It says, in effect: Although you imagine the mountains to be solid and without inward movement and growth, this is not the case. The mountains that seem stagnant and stationary to you are inwardly growing and changing, just like the clouds the motion of which is visible to you. The firm structure and development of all things are ensured by that same motion, the law of motion which is of God's creation and making. It prevails over all the particles and phenomena of nature, and it ensures their order and stability.

The choice of this particular wording in the Quran goes back, no doubt, to the fact that mountains are a symbol of bulkiness and stability, and it enables the verse to lay particular stress on the ability of the Creator to do all things.

Five, not more than three centuries have passed since Galileo presented to the world of science the theory of the motion of the earth, in a clear fashion and accompanied by adequate proof. In an age not too far removed from us, when geocentricity and the immobility of the earth were regarded as indubitable scientific principles, his theory met with a wave of furious opposition. By contrast, in the dark atmosphere of the Age of Ignorance, the Quran had already referred to certain aspects of the earth's motion and the mysterious qualities of mountains. This was an exposition of complex scientific truths, taking place already in that age. Thus the Quran says: *"Have We not made the earth as a cradle and the mountains like pegs?"* (78:6-7) *"God has placed mountains on the earth to prevent its uneven motion."* (31:10)

The Quran compares the earth to a cradle because a cradle is a place of rest that is engaged in motion. In another verse, a different comparison is offered: *"I have created the earth for you like a tamed camel that with its gentle and smooth motion does not vex its rider."* (67:15)

The Quran referred to the motion of the earth at a time when the Ptolemaic theory of geocentricity and the immobility of the earth had been ruling for centuries over the minds of the learned. It was the heavenly book of Islam that refuted that fantastic view of the world, almost a thousand years before Galileo.

In one of the verses just quoted, the mountains have been subtly and delicately compared to pegs that hold the earth in place and prevent it from becoming scattered. This is because the crust of the earth is covered with a soft layer of soil and sand, and were the earth to be deprived of firm and heavy mountains, it would undoubtedly lose its stability because of the pull exerted by the moon. It would fall prey to convulsion and shaking, and destructive tides would overwhelm the globe and destroy it.

The mountains serve as highly resistant pegs that play an essential role in preserving the earth from dissolution and destruction. The slight tremblings and convulsions that sometimes occur are not on a scale to deprive human life of all tranquility and stability.

Furthermore, the massive bulk of great mountains is able to neutralize and control, to a considerable extent, the powerful waves of molten materials and buried gases that emanate from within the earth. Were the mountains not to rear up their heads over our globe, the surface of the earth would be in constant ferment because of the pressure of molten substances, and its whole nature would change.

Therefore, bearing in mind that mountains are like pegs implanted in the earth, we realize that our tranquil and undisturbed existence on the globe is ensured precisely by the mountains.

The Quran similarly alludes to the earth being globular in shape, in the following verse: *"I swear by the Lord of the easts and the wests."* (70:40) It is obvious that a multiplicity of easts and wests— points at which the sun rises and sets. Every point of the globe is, at some moment, the east for a certain group of people, and the west for another group of people.

Do truths such as these not serve to make us better acquainted with the profound truths this heavenly book contains?

Six, the Quran describes the factors which give rise to milk in animals in a way that is entirely compatible with the data of modern science. This is what God's book has to say: *"There is in truth for you a lesson in your animals and flocks. We give you to drink a pure milk derived from that which is contained in their bodies, from the merging of what is held in their intestines with blood. The drinking of that is then made easy for those who drink it."* (16:16)

Dr. Bucaille writes in his book: "From a scientific point of view, physiological notions must be called upon to grasp the meaning of this verse. The substances that ensure the general nutrition of the body come from chemical transformations which occur along the length of the digestive tract. These substances come from the contents of the intestine. On arrival in the intestine at the appropriate stage of chemical transformation, they pass through its wall and towards the systemic circulation. This passage is effected in two ways: either directly, by what are called the 'lymphatic vessels', or indirectly, by the portal circulation. This conducts them first to the liver, where they undergo alterations, and from here they then emerge to join the systemic circulation. In this way everything passes through the bloodstream. The constituents of the milk are secreted by the mammary glands. These are nourished, as it were, by the product of food digestion brought to them via the bloodstream. Blood therefore plays the role of collector and conductor of what has been extracted from food, and it brings nutrition to the mammary glands, the producers of milk, as it does to any other organ.

"Here the initial process which sets everything else in motion is the bringing together of the contents of the intestine and blood at the level of the intestinal wall itself. This very precise concept is the result of the discoveries made in the chemistry and physiology of the digestive system. It was totally unknown at the time of the Prophet Muhammad and has been understood only in recent times. The discovery of the circulation of the blood, was made by Harvey roughly ten centuries after the Quranic Revelation.

"I consider that the existence in the Quran of the verse referring to these concepts can have no human explanation on account of the period in which they were formulated."[41]

Seven, it is only recently that researchers have come aware of insemination in plants and learned that every living being comes into existence as the result of the merging of a male and female cell.

Before the invention of the microscope, which gave man access to the world of atoms and enabled him to study microscopic beings, no one was aware of the action and reaction among male and female cells, certainly not in the Age of Ignorance, and indeed not until the codification of classical botany.

The numerous experiments and investigations by scientists in this field have proven that reproduction is impossible without insemination, except in certain plants where reproduction takes place by way of the division of cells.

The first person to analyze this scientific fact in a clear and straightforward fashion was the well-known Swedish scientist, Charles Leine (1707-1787).

Scientific information shows that reproduction among plants generally takes place through insemination with microscopic particles, and the agents of insemination are insects, flies, bees and so forth, together with the most effective and widespread agent of all—the wind, which lifts up nearly weightless particles and scatters them in the air.

In verses that are totally free of ambiguity, the Noble Quran sets forth clearly the principle of gender in the vegetable world, together with the existence of male and female cells in plants, something which was completely unknown until quite recently. It says, with the utmost eloquence: *"Do they not look at the earth, where We have created the plants in pairs?"*(42:7) *"We sent down water from the heavens, and made to grow thereby pairs of different species of plants."*(20:51) *"Pure and transcendent is the God Who created all contingent things in pairs—plants, human beings, and other forms of creation unknown to you."*(36:36)

After setting forth the principle of two genders in the human being, the animals and the plant world, the Quran enlarges the scope of the principle to the degree of embracing all parts of existence. It is a general rule and law to which nothing that can be called existent forms an exception. The Quran says: *"We have created all things their pair, in order that you may remember God."*(51:49)

Given the profound knowledge at the human being's disposal in the present age, he has come to realize that all substances in the world can be reduced, in the final analysis, to their smallest structural unit, the atom. This infinitely small unit itself comprises a duality: that of positive and negative electricity.

Although these two forces are identical with respect to their existential nature, one of them carries a positive electrical load and the other, a negative one. It is this opposition that attracts them to each other.

Attraction toward the opposite pole is inherent in both of them, and once the mutual attraction is exerted, a third entity comes into being—a force which is neutral in its electrical load.

It is very remarkable that the pairing of all things should have been mentioned in the Quran, which was, after all, revealed in an environment dominated by ignorance. The attraction that exists between two bodies each bearing a different kind of electric load makes entirely appropriate the use of the word "pair." for it is entirely similar to the attraction between the two opposite genders. "Pair" was an extremely effective way of describing this scientific reality, given the limited thoughts of men at the time and even later, for it is not until recently that clear and definite information about the physical nature of this matter became available.

So if we generalize the phenomenon of the pair to include the inner structure of atoms, we may conclude that the material structure of the world is indeed based on pairing, and that nothing in the material universe is exempt from the operation of this comprehensive principle.

Paul Ruybruck, an English scholar, says: "Each particle of matter is confronted by an opposing particle, as was proven in 1955. Using an atom breaker, physicists were able to discover counter-protons, counter-neutrons and counter-matters. They became convinced that the structure of the world of counter matter corresponds exactly to that fo the world of matter, and that the two always accompany each other."[42]

As Max Planck, another twentieth century scientist, puts it: "Every material body is compounded of electrons and protons."[43]

One of the findings of the natural and chemical sciences, proved by laboratory experiments, is that the roots of plants increase the volume of the earth. When water penetrates into bubbles inside the earth, the air that has accumulated there is driven further inside the earth, so that the depths of the earth begin to seethe in agitation.

When rainfall penetrates the depths fo the earth, the roots of plants begin to move and advance through the soil. It is obvious that numerous smaller and more delicate roots branch forth from the original roots, moving out in every direction. For example, the capillary roots of maize, each one square centimeter thick, may reach a total of 4200.

Scientists are of the opinion that roots derive 95% of their needs from the air and only 5% from the soil. Hence the amount of space occupied in the earth by roots is considerably expanded in its volume, so that the earth as a whole swells and becomes more capacious as a result of the growth of roots within it.

Let us look now at verse 5 of Surah Hajj in the Noble Quran: *"Look at the earth: first it is dry and devoid of vegetation, then We send rain down upon it, and it begins to stir and to swell and all kinds of beautiful plants start growing in it."*

This forms another example of the agreement of the Quran with modern science.

Eight, the Quran also mentions the role and operation of another factor in the bringing of things to fruition, the wind. *"We have sent the winds as a means of insemination and impregnation, and then sent down rain from the heavens."* (15:22)

In this verse, the Quran unveils another great mystery of creation, the fundamental role played by the wind in the fertilization of clouds. Using complex instruments and electrical means, civilized man has made great progress in recent years resulting in the establishment of the discipline known as meteorology. Specialists in this discipline point out the following: "It must be recognized that the obtaining of two conditions—the existence of steam in the air and its distillation to the point of saturating the air—is not enough to cause the formation of clouds and the occurrence of rainfall. A third condition is also necessary, which we may call fertilization."

Science confirms that winds is also a contributory factor in the fertilization of plants.

In the appearance of natural phenomena, a kind of friction and delay always exists. For example, if water is pure and stationary, it is possible that its temperature be reduced to below zero without its solidifying and that it not begin to boil until its temperature is much higher than 100 degrees. Also, steam may not begin to distil even though it has reached a point of saturation, and once it has distilled, its globules may be so minute that they do not fall, remaining instead suspended in the air so that no rainfall occurs. It is necessary for the wind to provide invisible particles of salt, picked up from the surface of the oceans, that then form nuclei of attraction and inflation. More importantly, the moisture in the air has to accumulate around the crystallized snowflakes that have formed at higher altitudes and are then scattered by the wind.

Finally, the minute initial drops of rain merge with each other as a result of the collision and intermingling of the winds until they gradually grow in size and fall through cloud masses as a result of their relatively great weight.

As a result of their friction with features of the earth and with bodies suspended in the air, cloud masses acquire opposing electrical forces. The release of this electricity is accompanied by intense friction of the particles in the air and the formation of nitrogen. This process contributes considerably to the merging and growing of raindrops and the occurrence of rainfall.

In short, the formation and strengthening of clouds, and the occurrence of rainfall and snow, cannot take place without a form of fertilization, accomplished through the intervention of an outside factor.

Artificial rainfall likewise depends on artificial fertilization, carried out in the following way: an airplane scatters "water dust" (pulverized and crystallized ice) in air that has the potentiality of cloud formation but is in a state of delayed equilibrium.

Discussing the rich treasury of knowledge contained in the Quran, Dr. Bucaille writes: "Whereas monumental errors are to be found in the Bible, I could not find a single error in the Quran. I had to stop and ask myself: if a man was the author of the Quran, how could he have written facts in the seventh century A.D. that today are shown to be in keeping with modern scientific knowledge? There was absolutely no doubt about it: the text of the Quran we have today is most definitely a text of the period, if I may be allowed to put it in these terms (in the next chapter of the present section of the book I shall be dealing with this problem). What human explanation can there be for this observation? In my opinion there is no explanation; there is no special reason why an inhabitant of the Arabian Peninsula should, at a time when King Dagobert was reigning in France (629-639 A.D.), have had scientific knowledge on certain subjects that was ten centuries ahead of our own."[44]

Lesson Sixteen
Prediction of the Defeat
of a Great Power

The beginning of the mission of the Most Noble Messenger came in the year 611 AD, and thus fell in the reign of Khusrau Parviz.

At that time, two great and powerful states, Eastern Rome or Byzantium and Iran, ruled over the greater part of the civilized world. They had for long been going to war with each other in order to expand the area under their control.[45] These lengthy battles between the Byzantines and the Iranians had begun in the reign of Anushirvan and had continued into the reign of Khusrau Parviz.

Encouraged and egged on by his advisors, Anushirvan had disregarded the peace treaty existing with Byzantines and attacked them. Within a short period, the Iranians succeeded in conquering Syria and Antioch, advancing as far as Asia Minor itself. Antioch was burned to the ground and Asia Minor was plundered. Twenty years later, when the military power of both sides was crumbling, a new peace agreement was signed, and the forces of both states returned to their previous borders.

After the death of Anushirvan and its aftermath, Khusrau Parviz ultimately came to the throne. In 614 AD he attacked the Greeks again, gaining control of Syria, Palestine and North Africa. He sacked Jerusalem, set fire to the Holy Sepulchre, and destroyed numerous cities. The war ended in a clear victory for Iran.

News of the defeat of the Byzantine worshippers of God, at the hands of the fire-worshipping Iranians, was received with satisfaction by the idolators of Mecca and with grief and sadness by the Muslims. In the course of this bloody struggle, Jerusalem had come into the possession of the Iranians, which was taken by the polytheists as a good omen for their own struggle against the Muslims, foretelling victory and triumph over them.

This interpretation made by the Meccans was grievous to the Muslims and caused them much anxiety about the future course of events. It was then that a revelation came foretelling the renewed triumph of the Byzantines, worshippers of God, over the Iranians; it disclosed the secret that the Byzantines would make good their defeat in less than ten years and carry off a definitive victory. These are the relevant verses of the Quran: *"The Byzantines have been defeated in a land near the Hijaz, but in the future they will triumph over their enemies, in a period of less than ten years. All affairs, both earlier and later, are in the hands of God, and on the day when the Byzantines triumph, the believers and the followers of Islam will rejoice. God assists whomsoever He wills, and He is powerful and compassionate. This is the promise of God, a promise which cannot be violated, but most of the people know not."*(30:1-6)

The prophesy of the Quran was fulfilled in the year 625 AD, corresponding to year 2 AH. Less than ten years had passed since the previous battle between the two powers, and the Byzantines were able to occupy Iran. It was so definite and certain for the Muslims that this event would take place that some of them placed bets on it like Abu Bakr who took out a bet against Ubayy b. Khalaf.[46]

How can we explain the confident and categorical prediction of the victory of a defeated people over a victorious people, in the absence of any factors pointing to the likelihood of such an event? A realistic approach to the state of society and the course of events would definitely have contradicted this prophesy.

The Prophet of Islam foretold a definite military victory at a certain point in the future; how did he know it was going to occur? Would it be fair to put it on the same level as the predictions made by politicians and political commentators? Could the application of any criteria have made it possible to calculate that a people, defeated, exhausted and demoralized in the course of a trying war, should within a given space of time, triumph definitively over the erstwhile victor? It should be remembered, after all, that many factors play a role in military victory and that the slightest error in tactics or miscalculation can change the whole course of battle.

Surely the explanation is that some unaccountable element is contained in the unfolding of events, which permits the prediction of an occurrence like a great military victory. It is unrealistic to attempt to analyze these matters from a purely materialistic point of view.

The Prediction of Other Events

The Quran has also foretold other events. Let us give a few examples. One is the conquest of Mecca and the triumph of the Muslims over the polytheists, described by the Quran as follows: *"That which God inspired in his Prophet by means of a dream is true and veracious: without any doubt, you will enter the Sacred Mosque in safety and security. You will shave your heads and shorten your hair without any fear or anxiety. God knows what you do not know, and you will win a victory near at hand before your conquest of Mecca."* (48:27)

This verse informs the Muslims that they will enter the Sacred Mosque and perform the ceremonies of the lesser pilgrimage (*'umra*) without any fear, and that the polytheists will be defeated and their power will vanish. It also assures them that in the near future they will enjoy another victory. These predictions were made at a time when no military expert or adviser could have predicted the occurrence, given the difficult circumstances of the Muslims and the unfavorable situation in which they found themselves.

In reality, then, it was not the outer beings of the Muslim warriors, the physical strength and weaponry they possessed, that were victorious; it was God's aid, joined to their strenuous efforts, that gave rise to victory .

The repeated statement in the Quran that all miracles and victories take place with the permission of God indicates how limited is the role played by personalities in history despite their power of choice and the dimensions their creative activity may assume.

The Prophets represent the most important of the factors necessary for destroying existing social realities and bringing about social changes at a given point in history. With their luminosity, they penetrate the darkness surrounding society that is an obstacle on the path to God. They create a distinctive set of values, and with God's permission, they guide men to righteousness and salubrity.

It is precisely within the growing darkness that the evolutionary course of history causes the emergence of exalted personalities. Their appearance is one of the basic factors in bringing about fundamental social change and one of the undoubted necessities of history.

A careful examination of history will show that the Prophets appeared at decisive turning points in time, playing a fundamental role in conveying human societies from a lower stage to a higher one. It is then up to the human being himself firmly to base his orientation to the world on an awareness of the constant evolution of all phenomena and the movement of all of being toward its lofty aims, as well as on faith and belief in the source of creation and worthy action that brings him into harmony with the universal proclamation of God's glory by all things. Only then will his true human visage as the vicegerent upon the earth become apparent. This proper orientation toward existence and the phenomena of nature will determine for him the values of his earthly existence.

History bears witness that human beings have joyously abandoned everything for the sake of the Divine teachings brought by the Prophets, in order to gain, thereby, that which is both everything and higher than everything.

Let us return to our previous topic.

The Quran mentions the future occurrence of another historical event, namely the triumph of the Muslim warriors at Khaybar and their conquest of its formidable fortresses. Hard blows had been inflicted on the Muslims from Khaybar, but in the end the army of Islam triumphed over the Jews, and the prediction of the Quran was completely fulfilled.

Would it have been possible to speak of victory, at a time of the utmost weakness, without utter confidence in the content of Divine revelation? Can we ascribe this precise knowledge of the future to the knowledge and perspicacity of the Prophet of Islam?

Knowledge cannot permit one to speak of an ineluctable future, to make categorical predictions; this is something in which only the true Prophets and friends of God can engage.

In these victorious wars, Islam triumphed not only materially over the forces of unbelief; it also subjected its opponents and enemies to its ideological and spiritual power.

When the Prophet was still living in Mecca and propagating

Islam on a limited scale in extremely difficult and tiring circumstances, and when the future of Islam was still uncertain, the Quran predicted the ultimate fate of Abu Lahab to be inevitable entry to hellfire on account of his obstinate enmity to the Prophet of Islam.

Although many of the relatives of the Prophet joined the ranks of his opponents at the beginning of his mission, their innate ability to perceive and accept the truth gradually emerged from the darkness of ignorance and obstinacy, so despite their obduracy and perversity of mind, they changed their beliefs and joined the ranks of the Muslims.

At that time of feverish cries, nobody knew who would ultimately join the ranks of the believers and which opponents of the truth would maintain their erroneous attitudes until death. After all, the passage of time, the occurrence of certain events and the emerging of new conditions can bring about new insights in the human being, with the result that he changes his beliefs an opinions; no one can foretell with certainty what the future beliefs of a person will be.

Nonetheless, the Quran predicts with clarity the final outcome of the life of a given individual, Abu Lahab, the obstinate enemy of Islam. It proclaims categorically that he will refuse the religion of monotheism until the very end of his life, and that for this reason his painful destiny will be to enter the fire of God's wrath. These are the verse of the Quran: "*May Abu Lahab, who was constantly vexing and opposing the Prophet, perish, and may his two hands be cut off! The wealth he accumulated to destroy Islam has not availed him or saved him from destruction; he will soon fall into the flaming fire of Hell.*" (111:1-3)

All historians are agreed that Abu Lahab closed his eyes on this world as an unbeliever and that he persisted in his obstinate hostility to the Prophet of Islam until the final moments of his life.

The verses revealed concerning the events mentioned above constitute a further proof that the sacred book of Islam is from God, and that it is linked, in a profound and exclusive way, with the supra-natural realm.

Other verses of the Quran also predict certain future events, such as the preservation of the Prophet from physical harm throughout the period of his messengerhood and his inhumanity from the evil deeds of his enemies. At the time this was predicted, the third year after the beginning of his mission, there was no indication that he would remain unharmed by his enemies throughout the period of his mission, and yet the passage of time proved this to be the case.

In *Surah Kawthar*, the Quran informs people that the descendants of the Prophet will ultimately be numerous—this despite the fact that in his lifetime his enemies were hopeful that he would die without issue, since all the sons of the Prophet had died in infancy and only one of his daughters survived. Given this, was it possible for any other than God, that eternal reality and fixed pivot of truth, to predict that matters would unfold in a sense completely opposed to existing circumstances? Likewise, the prediction that the Prophet would return to Mecca, his home, made at a time when he abandoned it for Medina because of the pressures of the polytheists, is also an indication of a higher consciousness: *"God Who made incumbent on you the recitation of the Quran will return you to your birthplace."* (28:85)

In *Surah Nasr*, the Quran also predicts the definitive conquest of Mecca by the Muslims with numerous different groups of people joining the ranks of the Muslims. All these predictions of future events are inexplicable unless they be ascribed to the source of revelation, to the infinite knowledge of God.

It should also not be forgotten that in all the wars and battles they waged and all the victories they won, the Muslims behaved toward the defeated with the utmost generosity and compassion. In this, they were guided by the inspiration they received from the Quran, an inspiration that took shape in the very midst of the battles and clashes in which they were engaged. Since the war waged by Islam was a war for the sake of God and the establishment of monotheism and justice, they never lost sight of the purpose of fighting even in the midst of battle and the clanging of swords.

Although military victory might have appeared to be the best possible opportunity for the Muslims to take revenge on the polytheists for all the pain and torture they had suffered at their hands for years, the Muslims restrained their anger and desire for revenge so that the sacred aim of their struggle should not be sullied or obscured by their personal desires and wishes.

Lesson Seventeen
Unity and Multiplicity
in the Themes of the Quran

Every scientist and researcher is liable to change his attitude to scientific topics under investigation and the opinions he bases on them. Relying on the knowledge and conclusions he has accumulated, he may express a certain opinion on a given topic at one time and later repudiate that opinion in the light of continuing and more extensive research and the solution of certain problems. His new insights take the place of his previous thinking, and his opinion changes. This process of change is an important reason for the variations and contradictions we find within the views of a single individual.

Furthermore, in the course of twenty-three years, a person will inevitably change some of his ideas and opinions as a result of natural bodily changes which also entail changes in his psychology and nervous system.

It has always been the custom of thinkers, lawgivers and writers to correct their errors and revise their opinions and their writings.

Moreover, when the human being is caught up in a current of great events, in a succession of differing circumstances, his view of matters cannot possibly remain uniform. However firm be his will and however balanced his thoughts, the stormy vicissitudes of existence will inevitably destroy the stability of his mind and his will and divert their operation to new courses.

When the human being is weak and impotent, he looks at the world in a certain way, but as soon as he attains a position of power, his view of the world changes and he confronts the same questions that faced him before in an entirely new way. This change in outlook can easily be seen reflected in his manner of speech and behavior.

This is another factor giving rise to contradiction and variation within the views and modes of thought of a single individual.

In addition, intelligent and perspicacious persons are well aware that those who deviate from the path of honesty always end up by unconsciously contradicting themselves, however cunningly they make their calculations. This is particularly true if they life in the same society for a number of years and express opinions on a whole variety of issues. It is the direct result of their deviation from the path of honesty.

The Noble Quran contains profound and exact statements on a wide variety of subjects. It establishes and legislates principles and regulations for the practical and ethical duties of the human being and for the ordering and administration of society. However, the slightest variation or contradiction is not to be seen in this great mass of material. Considering the fact that the Quran was revealed over a period of twenty-three years, it is important to note that this gradualness did not cause the verses to lose their harmony and inner unity.

It is true, of course, that certain verses containing regulations were abrogated by others, so that the period of their applicability came to an end. But the meaning of this abrogation is that the benefit envisioned by the regulation proclaimed in the earlier verse was temporally limited, so that the corresponding regulation also was necessarily limited. Once the new regulation is proclaimed, the validity of the first regulation is terminated. It is plain that the proclamation of a temporary regulation cannot be objected to if the benefit intended by a permanent regulation is not yet apparent.

This is something quite different from what happens as a result of human error and ignorance. The human being promulgates a certain regulation with a view to a certain benefit, and then, after a time, he realizes he has made a mistake. He then abolishes the first regulation and substitutes another one for it.

One cannot in any way attribute to God such an abrogation, arising from ignorance and error. Concerning the question of abrogation, the Noble Quran has this to say: "*Whenever We abrogate a certain benefit and send down another in its place—and God knows best what He sends down—the unbelievers say, 'You are always a forger.' It is not so, but most of them do not understand. Say, 'The Spirit of Sanctity has brought down these verses from my Lord, in truth and veracity, to make firm the footsteps of the believers on the path of God and to serve as guidance and good tidings for the Muslims.'*(27:101-102)

Here, it is possible to evaluate the Quran from two different points of view: first, the individual nature of the verses, viewed in isolation from each other and possessing an unparalleled brilliance; and second, the verses taken together as a whole, exhibiting utter harmony and mutual compatibility and lacking all contradiction with respect to style and content. Precisely this lack of contradiction represents another aspect of the miraculousness of the Quran.

When the Quran wishes to establish its own heavenly nature, it draws attention to the fact that although it was revealed over a period of twenty-three years, it is completely uniform and lacking in contradiction. It says: *"Do they not reflect on the Quran? If this book were from other than God, they would certainly find much variation and contradiction in it."*(4:81)

This verse reminds us that those who deviate from the path of honesty and veracity will naturally fall prey to contradiction in their statements and sayings. The fact that not the slightest trace of contradictoriness can be found in the contents of the Quran or unevenness in its style is a shining proof of its truth and veracity. The Quran therefore leaves it to the sound disposition of human beings, untrammeled by all prejudices and pre-existing notions, to recognize this fact and to distinguish truth from falsehood.

When we leaf through the history of the Prophet of Islam, we see clearly that his life passed through many different stages.

At one time he belonged to a deprived and impoverished minority; at another time, great material facilities and abundant wealth were at his disposal. At one time, his weakness and isolation and the social boycott imposed upon him were of an intensity sufficient to defeat the most powerful of human beings; at another time, he enjoyed such honor and fame that he counted as the leader of one of the strongest nations of the age. Sometimes he was confronted by the crises of war and all the disorders attending on war; at other times, he lived in an atmosphere of peace and tranquility.

We know that the changing conditions of life have a great

effect on the way human beings think and relate to each other and to nature. They represent such a dominant factor that they are able to bring about fundamental changes in their attitudes, to the extent that both their inner and outer lives are directly related to the changing nature of the circumstances that surround them. The changing circumstances specific to each stage in the human being's life create within him a certain way of viewing the world and a certain network of relationships. Among other things, this makes it possible for him to benefit from exceptional circumstances.

The positions human beings adopt with respect to all these changing circumstances is by no means uniform. Sometimes they are able to make use of them as a means for development and growth and the creation of values, and at other times those circumstances become transformed into ideals. By adopting a particular attitude to the external phenomena surrounding them, and choosing a certain approach with regard to the purpose of their existence within the overall scheme of creation, human beings give shape and form to their own existential nature.

In short, the life of this world, with its vast dimensions and variegated manifestations, determines the values of human beings, and clarifies their choice of direction.

If the Quran which took shape under a variety of different circumstances and was revealed in fragments over a period of twenty-three years, in Mecca and Medina, was the record of the thoughts of Muhammad (upon whom be peace and blessings), it would inevitably have been subject to the general rule that development implies change and contradiction; it would not possess the uniformity that it manifestly does.

Furthermore, through the adoption of an attitude conformable to the prevailing conditions of the day, considerable differences would have appeared within the worldview expounded in the Quran. Contradiction and incongruity would have become evident in it, and it would have lost, in the course of time, the evenness and harmony that characterize its style.

In contrast with the method followed by conventional books that devote themselves to explaining or researching a single legal, historical, philosophical, social or literary topic, the Quran discusses numerous and varied subjects, such as law and politics, the knowledge of God, civil and penal law, ethics and customs of behavior, history and the details of Divine regulations, together with tens of other subjects. Despite this, it is absolutely uniform with respect to the coherence of its subject matter and of its style. There is no difference between the first surah revealed to the Prophet (*Surah Alaq*) and the last surah of the Quran (*Surah Nasr*). Throughout the Quran, unique eloquence and power of expression are fully apparent, to the point of constituting a firm and brilliant proof in their own right.

The Quran represents a seamless and harmonious entity: none of its laws and principles can be viewed in isolation from all of its other laws and principles, and the examination of one principle may furnish a key for the understanding of other principles.

The inter-relatedness of the philosophical and moral foundations of the Quran, its laws and regulations for the life of the individual and society, its prescriptions for worship and the training of human beings, and the principles and moral purposes it sets out for administering society—this inter-relatedness is another clear proof of the miraculous nature of the Quran.

In none of the ordinances and principles expounded in the Quran do we see any contradiction with the creedal, philosophical, educational or ethical bases of the Quran. Despite all their varied aspects, none of the ordinances of the Quran are incompatible with its fundamental teachings.

These exceptional qualities and properties of the Quran form an indisputable proof of its superiority to all the products of human thought. They establish clearly that this inimitable compendium has its source in God, the eternal and immutable reality, Whose infinite essence is utterly beyond the factors that induce change, variation and contradiction.

Lesson Eighteen
The Inexhaustibility of the
Different Dimensions of the Quran

The Quran is a book which has brought about the greatest and most astounding changes in the history of the human being. It possesses an everlasting vitality and shines continuously throughout every age of history. With the profound insight it exhibits in legislating for the human being and providing for all his genuine and natural needs, it is the richest and most abundant resource available to the human being. The comprehensive scheme proposed by Islam rests on a perception of his primordial nature. With a realism that is all its own, Islam analyzes the human being as he is and assumes a determining role in all the dimensions of his life. This is one of the reasons for the lasting validity of Islam.

Taking into account the extensive developments that have occurred in science, bringing in their wake fundamental and irreversible changes, the characteristics that set Islam apart from other schools of thought must be examined with great care.

Were the principles and regulations of Islam to belong to the same category as those of other schools, the ascending level of the knowledge of human beings would necessarily invalidate them. But we see exactly the opposite is true. In circles that concern themselves with scientific and legal problems, the position of Islam is stronger than ever before; it enjoys increasing prestige and receives more attention than at any other time.

One of the clear characteristics of the Quran is that by means of a finite verbal form, it expresses an infinity of meaning that derives from the infinite knowledge of God. This is in contrast with all other books and writings where both the verbal form and the meanings they express are finite.

Imam Sadiq, upon whom be peace, said to Hammad: " 'I swear by God that I am aware of all that is in the heavens and the earth, and all that is in Paradise and hellfire.' Hammad then looked at the Imam with astonishment, whereupon he continued: 'Oh Hammad, it is by means of the Book of God that I have this knowledge.' He then recited this verse: *'On the day that We raise up a witness for every people from among their own messengers and bring you forth as a witness for this people. We have sent this great Quran to you to make plain the reality of all things and to be a source of guidance, mercy and glad tidings for the Muslims.' "*[47]

One of the companions of Imam Sadiq, upon whom be peace, related that he heard the Imam say: "I swear by God that I have in my possession all the truths of the Quran, from beginning to end. This book contains an account of the heavens and the earth, of that which is and that which has been, for the Quran makes apparent the reality of all things."

The Quran may be regarded as a transcript of the world of nature, the hidden secrets of which the passage of time and the expansion of knowledge have brought to light. The appearance of new and profound concepts in the Quran is therefore a continuing process.

God made His Book comprehensible so that human beings might reflect on it. Nonetheless, the secrets and mysteries of its verses become more apparent, and its rays exert a more powerful attraction, the more the scientific capacity of the human being increases and his researches concerning the scheme of the universe continue to expand. This is true also of researches into the psychology of the human being and the laws governing social and legal relationships. Thus thinkers who spend their lives studying exclusively civil or international law will never be able to reach the lofty pinnacle of the Quran.

As Ali, the Master of the Pious, said, "The Quran is a burning torch, the light of which will never be extinguished; it is a deep ocean, the depths of which will never be penetrated by human thought."[48]

From the dawn of Islam, scholars and believers have applied their lofty intellects to the study of the Quran in order to understand its various verses. In each age, hundreds of specialists have worked on the concepts of the Quran, each according to his degree of talent, and they have carved out paths for attaining knowledge of the Quran. Even in non-Islamic environments, some people have engaged in careful researches to bring out the meaning of the Quran, and the results they have attained have played an influential role in the dissemination of Islamic culture. These properties and attributes belong exclusively to the Quran, the value system of which is regarded as a precious legacy for all of mankind.

The unparalleled comprehensiveness of the Quran, when compared with other systems of legislation in the advanced and civilized world, is entirely apparent. It is here that we discover the vast difference between the Quran that was revealed to purify the human being and enable him to ascend, and the other source of legislation in the world. In countries where reliance is placed on those sources, laws are established with the aim of establishing human happiness but only through drawing on the abstract and imaginary ideas of thinkers and specialists in the field of law, in the hope that a fitting answer to all the material and spiritual needs of the human being might thus be provided.

But since those laws take into consideration only objective and external aspects of human life and fail to confront a whole series of fundamental realities, to such a degree that motive is sometimes regarded as being dictated by material circumstances; and since, moreover, they take no account of the norms that prevail in the human being's inner being, they yield undesirable results and prove to be defective cone put into practice, despite their apparent soundness. Their modification and revision then become inevitable.

No one can claim that his scientific writings and researches or his technical innovations will remain unsurpassed in every age, for progress and development make it inevitable that with the passage of time, scientific research should enter new channels and both theory and practice change fundamentally.

Indeed, each individual scientist will revise his ideas and his works as the degree of his knowledge increases and the level of his awareness improves. He will seek to compensate for previous deficiencies. The door is always open for such revisions and corrections.

Furthermore, every human work, however valuable and precise, is of ultimately limited utility: its value is finite, such that a few experts and specialists learned in their trade will be able to clarify every part of the book and exhaust its contents.

But the Noble Quran is revelation, deriving from the knowledge of a Creator in Whose infinite ocean of wisdom all the intelligence, thoughts and perceptions of human beings are but a drop; compared to the blinding brilliance of the vision and knowledge that embrace all of being, they are like a feeble and flickering lamp. The potentialities of the Quran for further investigation, discovery, and deduction are endless. This principle is not restricted to questions of law and jurisprudence; researchers in every branch of human knowledge can discover some new dimension of the Quran.

Even specialists in some of the modern sciences of the human being, such as psychology, sociology and the philosophy of history, can deduce new and exact points of scientific validity from the Quran. This shows that the Quran has a whole series of different capacities that cannot be exhausted by the imagination of a single culture or a single age. There is no other book on the general and particular aspects of which so much effort has been expended for fourteen centuries across such a vast area and which yet retains the capacity to be investigated still further.

It is obvious that the results obtained by thought and investigation will depend on the originality, skill and intellectual power of the individual scholar, so that the multi-dimensional meanings of the verses of the Quran cannot be restricted to what one individual has been able to deduce from them.

We should study carefully the topics contained in the Quran such as the origin of beings, the ineluctable future that is the afterlife, ethics, jurisprudence, law and historical narratives. Our aim is such a study should be more than a simple re-telling of events, a dry summary of contents; we should try to discover how the Quran has impelled human beings to advance intellectually from one stage to the next. Then we will encounter the true teachings of the Quran, and by opening up new fields of new knowledge and enquiry, we will come to appreciate the unique richness and profoundity of the Quran.

The spiritual, cultural and scientific richness of the Quran is such that if we tried to establish a kind of statistical bibliography for works written on the Quran including commentaries on the entire text, commentaries on its legal verses, and commentaries on certain *surahs*, the total would run into the tens of thousands.

Can this unique comprehensiveness of the Quran be explained by attributing it to the mind of a man who had never studied and who lived in an age of darkness and in one of the most backward of all countries—the Arabian Peninsula? Does anyone exist, even in today's world, who is capable of drawing up such a detailed and comprehensive program as that which Islamic law provides, a program moreover which is not purely abstract and theoretical but includes among its effects the spiritual ascent of the human being and the moral purity of society?

When we speak of the miraculousness of the Quran, we are not speaking on the basis of speculation or mere personal opinion, nor are we talking of something legendary or of purely historical significance. We base ourselves on scientific, rational and logical criteria, for the miraculousness of the Quran is a palpable truth comprehensible to any person of intelligence who has at his disposal the necessary information. Such a person will easily see the Quran is connected to a power superior to that of the human being.

Can all these unique properties and features of the Quran, which have retained their scientific significance and value for many centuries after the revelation, be regarded as something natural or commonplace? Or are they, on the contrary, a clear proof that the Quran, possessing these attributes to an infinite degree as it does, is to be ascribed to the Creator Who possesses Himself infinite existence?

Bartholeme Heller, a French Orientalist, discusses the comprehensiveness of the Quran in the following terms: "Just as we are obliged to appreciate the beauty and eloquence of the Quran by means of a translation, we also appreciate the beauty of the Psalms and the Vedas by means of a translation. There is, however, this difference: the Psalms do not contain a code of civil laws for the Jews, nor the Vedas for the Hindus, whereas the Quran contains an unparalleled variety of subject matter. The Quran is both a hymn in praise of God and a code of civil law; it is both prayer and supplication, and a warning and and exhortation. It teaches both the methods of warfare and those of debate, and it is a book of history and stories."[49]

In 1951, the College of Law in Paris organized a week long

seminar on Islamic jurisprudence in which the views of Islamic law on a variety of subjects were examined. The following communique was issued at the end of the seminar: "Islamic jurisprudence undoubtedly deserves to be regarded as one of the principal sources of law in the world. The views and opinions of the different schools of Islamic law contain abundant resources which are truly astounding and which can be drawn on by Islamic jurists to furnish answers to all the questions of modern life."

The Permanent Attraction Exerted by the Quran

Another aspect of the Quran which serves to indicate its unique and exceptional nature is the remarkable and inexhaustible attraction that it exerts. Take the best poems or pieces of literature, and read them several times. You will come to see that for all the interest you have in reading them and all the pleasure they give you, a repeated reading of them will tire and even bore you in the end.

The effectiveness and attractiveness of the best writings produced by geniuses of the past and present is not something fixed, immutable, and permanent. For a time, they can hold the reader under their sway but they will gradually forfeit their attractiveness so that in the end they can neither command attention nor cause any pleasure.

However, if we examine the Quran, this transcript of a heavenly archetype, from this point of view, we will see that those who are acquainted with the Quran and have acquired some of the riches contained in its teaching are well aware that there is a direct relationship between the repeated reading of the Quran and the attraction that it exerts. They read or recite God's verses hundreds of times, and each time the Quran acquires a different aspect for them, an aspect that conquers and overwhelms their soul and their spirit.

Their experience of spiritual pleasure is in direct proportion to their comprehension of the exalted concepts fo the Quran, and indeed anyone can satisfy his spiritual needs by referring constantly to the Quran and benefiting from it to the degree of his capacity to know and perceive.

The rays of attraction exerted by the Quran spread outwards from Mecca together with the movement of the Muslims. They shone in the Christian court of Ethiopia, thanks to the recitation of Ja'far b. Abi Talib, despite the unfavorable situation prevailing there and the pressure brought to bear by the opponents of Islam. Equally, they shone in Medina, the base for the formation of a new society, where the Quran was recited by Mus'qab b. 'Umayr.

Active people such as these were dedicated to destroying false values and bringing into being a movement that would result in fundamental changes in the way of life and thought and society. They sought to spread awareness among human beings and to encourage them to adopt a realistic attitude towards the truths of the Quran.

With its message, the Quran provided human beings with the means needed for making a choice between falsehood, on the one hand, and the new values that were enabling human beings to refashion their lives, on the other. For the life of the human being has no meaning unless he adheres to a certain worldview, a vision of existence and history, and a concept of the aim of creation.

Today, more than fourteen centuries after the revelation of the Quran, the captivating sound of the recitation of the Quran can still be heard in different parts of the world.

From buildings in cities and villages, from tents in the desert, from places of temporary lodging, along the routes where people travel, at every hour and minute of the day and in the heart of the night when all things are veiled in a profound and meaningful silence, the profoundly moving sound of the Quran being recited arises, leaving its impression on hearts and minds that have been attuned to its message and transforming fundamentally the spirits of all who listen to it. This happens continually without the Quran losing any of its freshness.

Although the Quran becomes intermingled with the various affairs and concerns of the human being's life as well as his emotions, it has always been immune against distortion and corruption.

If human knowledge and artifice had played any role in the codification of the Quranic text, the Quran would have resembled works of human origination that are always capable of being improved on at a later stage of development; for a time they possess a particular excellence, but they exert little effect on history and the ultimate destiny of the human being. They become obsolete, and the passage of time places the seal of death on them. But God, Whose power and knowledge are infinite, has so adorned the Quran with harmonious and well-ordered speech that it always preserves its freshness and eternal validity.

The mission of the Quran is to plant the seed of monotheism with all of its dimensions everywhere in the history and civilization of the human being. It is eloquent and categorical in conveying its message; it negates all forms of purposelessness in the human being's existence and condemns superficiality, shortsightedness, which necessarily fail to lead the human being to reality.

As for the teachings of the Quran concerning the knowledge of God, they so draw the truth-seeking spirit of the human being to the exalted concepts they expound that it rises up far above the values of the material world and fixes its gaze on horizons where new dimensions of reality become visible.

God Who presents the Quran to mankind is a unique force who cannot be compared with any created being. The norms He has established rule over all the phenomenal world, and in His infinity, He cannot be contained within the conceptual world. The Quran proclaims: *"He is God, the One without like; He is all-hearing and all-seeing."*(42:10)

We know that all existing things can be classified either as matter or as energy, and the Quran refutes clearly the possibility that the exalted essence of God be compared either to matter or to energy. This is the categorical statement of the Quran: *"No eye can perceive Him, but He observes all eyes; He is subtle and invisible, and well-aware of all things."*(6:103)

The Quran guides the human being to reflect carefully on the scheme of creation, to ponder deeply the inner nature of the bounties with which he has been blessed as well as the phenomena which surround him. A believer who travels through creation and reflects on the purposiveness of phenomena and contemplates the inner and outer aspects both of his own being and of his surroundings will reach the conclusion that all things are advancing—each by means of its specific path—toward a certain goal. If the human being wishes to attain his own salvation, he must conform to this universal tendency of all phenomena and join the caravan that is proceeding to the meeting with God.

The Noble Quran regards awareness of God as something innate in the human being, deriving from the very essence of the laws that govern creation. It depicts materialists and atheists as being caught up in a realm of mental abstraction and struggling against their innate disposition to seek God.

Similarly, all kinds of deviation from the path of monotheism, whether it be the dualism of Zoroastrianism or the Trinitarianism of Hinduism and Christianity (for the followers of Christianity imported the belief in the trinity into their faith from other religions), are condemned by the Quran. It regards all such deviations as attempts to conceal the truth: *"Those who say that God is one among three are unbelievers."*(5:73)

When condemning the belief that Ezra and Jesus were sons of God, the Quran describes this belief as a remnant of the beliefs held by ancient peoples: *"The Jews and the Christians say that Ezra and Jesus were the sons of God. This is what they say with their tongues, following those who were unbelievers before them."*(9:30)

The Quran makes this clear proclamation to the Prophet: *"Say: All praise belongs to God Who has never taken a son or a partner and Whose might and power can never diminish so that He might stand in need of a friend or a helper. Always praise the Divine Essence with mention of the greatest attributes of perfection."*(17:111)

Finally, in a short *surah*, the Quran thoroughly refutes the false thinking that underlies polytheism as follows: *"Say: He is God, the One; He is not empty of content; He is not the offspring of anyone, nor is anyone His offspring; nor is anyone like unto Him."*(112)

The statement that God is "not empty of content" (this being one of the possible meanings of *samad*) may relate to the fact that matter is hollow, generally speaking; there is a remarkable vacuum at the hearts of the atoms that make up the material world. This *surah* may thus be proclaiming that not belonging to the category of matter, God is "not empty of content."

Paul Clarence Ebersold, a physicist, poses this question: "Is God a person? Some people might reply that he is, but I do not think this scientifically correct. Scientifically speaking, we cannot form a material concept of God, for He exists beyond the realm of material perception. It is true, on the other hand, that numerous phenomena prove His existence; the works of His creation show clearly that He possesses infinite intelligence, knowledge and power."[50]

Weinhold, a well-known chemist, writes: "God does not represent some finite, material energy. Our limited ability to experiment and conceptualize is incapable of defining Him. Belief in the existence of God is a matter of the heart, although science may prove Him to be the prime and ultimate cause and thus indirectly reinforce the belief of the heart."[51]

This is how the logic of science approaches the question of describing the existence of the Creator. That which the Quran says concerning His unique essence is, therefore, in exact conformity with the highest truths of science.

The true value and significance of the fully rational teachings of the Quran concerning God become particularly apparent when we adopt a comparative approach in examining the relevant verses of the Quran. We could compare them, for example, with the teachings of Ancient Greece, the beliefs of Buddhism or Zoroastrianism or those held by the Arabs in the Age of Ignorance, for each of these covered a considerable portion of the world at that time.

A neutral and objective comparison of this kind would enable us to appreciate better the value of the conscious belief preached by Islam, a belief based on pure monotheism in all of its aspects and aimed at channelling all human activities toward a single goal. Such a comparison would also help us to understand more fully the miraculous nature of the Quran as an abundant source of truth, first made available to us more than fourteen centuries age.

No one who is armed with the weapon of religion and is fully conscious of the true teachings of Islam will form attachment to anything apart from his faith and whatever he needs to attain his high goals.

Lesson Nineteen
The Proclamation by Jesus of the Mission of the Prophet of Islam

There is no doubt that belief in the preceding Prophets is one of the pillars of the Islamic creed. The long line of Prophets who succeeded each other throughout history with the single goal of teaching the human being monotheism may be compared to a chain in which the final and most sublime link was the Most Noble Prophet of Islam.

If the Quran insists on the exalted position that God's messengers occupy in the history of revelation and calls on the Muslims to believe in the heavenly books that they brought, it is in order to confirm the truth and veracity of religion and to demonstrate that human beings must at all times turn to pure, authentic religions that derive from revelation, the religious guidance of humanity being entrusted by God in every age to a particular Prophet.

If we see any variation in the procedures and programs followed by the various Prophets, it is to be explained in terms of the swift changes that take place in human development and the passage of the human being from one stage to the next. For all the Prophets were, without distinction, true guides of humanity to the goals set by God; they preached a single doctrine deriving from a single source, advancing it in accordance with the dictates and circumstances of their time. The Quran says: "*We make no distinction among any of the Prophets.*"(2:135)

The sending of the Prophets formed part of the plan of creation from the very beginning, and the chain of the Messengers represented the gradual unfolding of Divine guidance. Just as the human being advanced in the general conduct of his life, so, too, the mission of the Prophets moved forward, in harmony with the progress of the human being, and the Prophets accordingly fore-told the appearance of the Prophets who would succeed them.

The Prophet of Islam confirmed the messengerhood of previous Prophets and the heavenly books they had brought, just as they had confirmed the Prophets who had preceded them. Those earlier Prophets had also proclaimed that others would follow them, so that the very leaders of religion clearly proclaimed the interconnectedness of all true religion.

Although the fact that the appearance of a Prophet has been foretold cannot serve in itself as proof for the veracity of a person's claim to prophethood, it does serve to indicate what might be the nature of a true Prophet and what qualities might be observed in him.

Were a name to be specified when predicting the emergence of a Prophet, this would, of course, be open to misuse, since naming is a conventional matter and anyone could adopt the name in question.

Similarly, to specify the exact moment when the Prophet was to appear would have facilitated the task of false claimants by giving them the opportunity to prepare themselves for making their fateful and monstrous claim. Furthermore, this might have led to a profusion of claims, which would then have induced confusion in the minds of people.

It may not be difficult for people with the ability to examine matters carefully and realistically to tell the difference between a true Messenger of God and false and erroneous claimants. But at the same time, it should not be forgotten that recognizing the truth, particularly in circumstances where it is mixed with falsehood, is not easy for those many people whose level of thought and awareness is not especially high. Many are those who fall into traps laid by the ambitions of the wicked.

It is for these reasons that the characteristics of a future Prophet are spelled out, these being the distinctive signs by which he may be recognized. Then those scholars on whom others depend for guidance in this matter can measure the claimant to prophethood against the characteristics that have been mentioned, devoting themselves to the task in utter purity and sincerity.

Christianity never advanced the claim that the religion of Jesus would be permanent and eternal or that Jesus was the Seal of the

Prophets and a guarantor of the textual integrity of the Gospels. Other religions also did not make analogous claims for themselves.

Islam does, however, speak of being the last and most perfect of all religions and of its Messenger being the Seal of the Prophets. It therefore follows that the heavenly book of Islam must always be protected from corruption and distortion.

The fundamental difference between the sacred books of Christianity and Islam is that Christianity lacks a revealed text that was fixed at the very time of its origins, whereas Islam possesses one.

The Gospels which we now have at our disposal have been extensively criticized by scholars and researchers who have examined different copies of the Gospels and have reached the conclusion that the New Testament has undergone many changes. There are many indications that the text of the Gospels has been codified to a considerable extent, to conform to personal beliefs and opinions.

John Nass, a historian of religions, writes as follows: "The history of Christianity is the story of a religion that arose from a belief in Divine incarnation having taken place in the person of its founder. All the teachings of Christianity revolve around the conviction that the person of Jesus represents the clearest manifestation of the Divine essence. But this religion that started out with a belief in Divine incarnation was transformed through a series of developments and took on a human dimension so that all the weaknesses and imperfections of the human condition began to appear in it.

"The story of religion is extremely long, including many ups and downs and moments of both glory and shame; it is these contrasts that give it meaning and significance. In none of the world's religions have such exalted spiritual aims been manifest as in Christianity; but equally in none of them has the failure to reach those aims been so marked."

Despite the textual corruption to which the Gospels have been subject, there are indications that the expressions "Spirit of Truth," "Holy Ghost" and "Comforter" which they contain may refer to the Prophet of Islam.

The Gospels record that Jesus addressed his disciples as follows: "Hereafter I will not talk much with you: for the prince of this world cometh, and hath nothing in me.[52] But when the Comforter is come, whom I will send unto you from the Father, even the Spirit of truth, which proceedeth from the Father, he shall testify of me."[53] "Nevertheless, I tell you the truth: It is expedient for you that I go away: for if I go not away, the Comforter will not come unto you; but if I depart, I will send him unto you. And when he is come, he will reprove the world of sin, and of righteousness and of judgment: of sin, because they believe not on me; of righteousness because I go to my Father, and you see me no more; of judgment because the prince of this world is judged. I have yet many things to say unto you but ye cannot bear them now. Howbeit, when he, the Spirit of truth is come, he will guide you into all truth: for he shall not speak of himself; but whatsoever he shall hear, that shall he speak; and he will shew you things to come. He shall glorify me, for he shall receive of mine and shall shew it unto you."[54] "But the Comforter, which is the Holy Ghost, whom the Father will send in my name, he shall teach you all things, and bring all things to your remembrance, whatsoever I have said unto you."[55]

If we say that the Comforter is identical with the Holy Ghost, we know that the Holy Ghost constantly accompanied Jesus and it would therefore not have been correct for him to say: "He will not come to you until I go."

When the Prophet Jesus says, "The prince of the world cometh" and that he will guide mankind, he is in effect accepting the religion to be brought by that person as the most perfect of all religions. Can the description of him given by Jesus fit anyone other than Muhammad, upon whom be peace and blessings?

When Jesus says, "He shall testify of me," and "he shall glorify me," did anyone other than the Prophet of Islam revere and honor Jesus or defend the innocence of Mary against the unworthy accusations made by the Jews?

Was it the Holy Ghost that did these things, or the Prophet of Islam? In addition to the fact that these verses clearly bear witness that the Comforter, the Holy Ghost, the Spirit of truth, cannot be anyone other than the Prophet of Islam, we also encounter the world "Paraclete" in some of the Gospels, the meaning of which is identical with that of the named Muhammad and Ahmad. Translators of the Gospels however have taken the work *perikletos*, a proper name in Greek equivalent in its meaning to Ahmad, to be *parakletos*, translating this as "Comforter."

Dr. Bucaille has a valuable discussion of this subject in the Chapter called "Jesus's Last Dialogues. The Paraclete of John's Gospel." "John is the only evangelist to report the episode of the last dialogue with the Apostles. It takes place at the end of the Last Supper and before Jesus's arrest. It ends in a very long speech: four chapters in John's Gospel (14 to 17) are devoted to this narration which is not mentioned anywhere in the other Gospels. These chapters of John nevertheless deal with questions of prime importance and fundamental significance to the future outlook. They are set out with all the grandeur and solemnity that characterizes the farewell scene between the Master and His disciples.

"This very touching farewell scene which contains Jesus's spiritual testament is entirely absent from Matthew, Mark and Luke. How can the absence of this description be explained? One might ask the following: did the text initially exist in the first three Gospels? Was it subsequently suppressed? Why? It must be state immediately that no answer can be found; the mystery surrounding this huge gap in the narrations of the first three evangelists remains as obscure as ever.

"The dominating feature of this narration—seen in the crowning speech—is the view of man's future that Jesus describes, His care in addressing His disciples and through them the whole of humanity, His recommendations and commandments and His concern to specify the guide whom man must follow after His departure. The text of John's Gospel is the only one to designate him as *parakletos* in Greek which in English has become Paraclete. The following are the essential passages:

"If you love me, you will keep my commandments. And I will pray the Father, and he will give you another Paraclete." (14, 15-16)

"What does 'Paraclete' mean? The *present* text of John's Gospel explains its meaning as follow:

"But the Paraclete, the Holy Spirit, whom the Father will send in my name, he will teach you all things, and bring to your remembrance all that I have said to you." (14, 26).

"...he will bear witness to me..." (15, 26)

"It is to your advantage that I go away, for if I do not go away, the Paraclete will not come to you; but if I go, I will send him to you. And when he comes, he will convince the world of sin and of righteousness and of judgment..." (16, 7-8)

"When the Spirit of truth comes, he will guide you into all the truth; for he will not speak on his own authority, but whatever he hears he will speak, and he will declare to you the things that are to come. He will glorify me..." (16, 13-14).

"(It must be noted that the passages in John, chapters 14-17, which have not been cited here, in no way alter the general meaning of these quotations).

On a cursory reading, the text which identifies the Greek work 'Paraclete' with the Holy Spirit is unlikely to attract much attention. This is especially true when the subtitles of the text are generally used for translations and the terminology commentators employ in works for mass publication direct the reader towards the meaning in these passages that an exemplary orthodoxy would like them to have. Should one have the slightest difficulty in comprehension, there are many explanations available such as those given by A. Tricot in his *Little Dictionary of the New Testament* (*Petit Dictionnaire du Nouveau Testament*) to enlighten one on this subject. In his entry on the Paraclete this commentator writes the following:

" 'This name or title translated from the Greek is only used in the New Testament by John: he uses it four times in his account of Jesus's speech after the Last Supper [56] (14, 16 and 26; 15, 26; 16, 7) and once in his First Letter (2, 1). In John's Gospel the word is applied to the Holy Spirit; in the Letter it refers to Christ. "Paraclete" was a term in current usage among the Hellenist Jews, First century A.D., meaning "intercessor," "defender" (...) Jesus predicts that the Spirit will be sent by the Father and Son. Its mission will be to take the place of the Son in the role he played during his mortal life as a helper for the benefit of his disciples. The Spirit will intervene and act as a substitute for Christ, adopting the role of Paraclete or omnipotent intercessor.'

"This commentary therefore makes the Holy Spirit into the ultimate guide of man after Jesus's departure. How does it square with John's text?

"It is a necessary question because *a priori* it seems strange to ascribe the last paragraph quoted above to the Holy Spirit: 'for he will not speak on his own authority, but whatever he hears he will speak, and he will declare to you the things that are to come.' It seems inconceivable that one could ascribe to the Holy Spirit the ability to speak and declare whatever he hears...Logic demands that this question be raised, but to my knowledge, it is not usually the subject of commentaries.

"To gain an exact idea of the problem, one has to go back to the basic Greek text. This is especially important because John is universally recognized to have written in Greek instead of another language. The Greek text consulted was the *Novum Testamentum Graece*.[57]

"Any serious textual criticism begins with a search for variations. Here it would seem that in all the known manuscripts of John's Gospel, the only variation likely to change the meaning of the sentence is in passage 14, 26 of the famous Palimpsest version written in Syriac.[58] Here it is not the Holy Spirit that is mentioned, but quite simply the Spirit. Did the scribe merely miss out a word or, knowing full well that the text he was to copy claimed to make the Holy Spirit hear and speak, did he perhaps lack the audacity to write something that seemed absurd to him? Apart from this observation there is little need to labour the other variations, they are grammatical and do not change the general meaning. The important thing is that what has been demonstrated here with regard to the exact meaning of the verbs 'to hear' and 'to speak' should apply to all the other manuscripts of John's Gospel, as is indeed the case.

The verb 'to speak' in the translation is the Greek verb 'laleo' which has the general meaning of 'to emit sounds' and the specific meaning of 'to speak'. This verb occurs very frequently in the Greek text of the Gospels. It designates a solemn declaration made by Jesus during His preachings. It therefore becomes clear that the communication to man which He here proclaims does not in any way consist of a statement inspired by the agency of the Holy Spirit. It has a very obvious material character moreover, which comes from the idea of the emission of sounds conveyed by the Greek word that defines it.

"The two Greek verbs 'akouo' and 'laleo' therefore define concrete actions which can only be applied to a being with hearing and speech organs. It is consequently impossible to apply them to the Holy Spirit.

"For this reason, the text of this passage from John's Gospel, as handed down to us in Greek manuscripts, is quite incomprehensible if one takes it as a whole, including the words 'Holy Spirit' in passage 14, 26: "But the Paraclete, the Holy Spirit, whom the Father will send in my name" etc. It is the only passage in John's Gospel that identifies the Paraclete with the Holy Spirit.

"If the words 'Holy Spirit" (*to pneuma to agion*) are omitted from the passage, the complete text of John then conveys a meaning which is perfectly clear. It is confirmed moreover, by another text by the same evangelist, the First Letter, where John uses the same word 'Paraclete' simply to mean Jesus, the intercessor at God's side.[59] According to John, when Jesus says (14, 16): 'And I pray the Father, and he will give you another Paraclete,' what He is saying is that 'another intercessor will be sent to man, as He Himself was at God's side on man's behalf during His earthly life.

"According to the rules of logic therefore, one is brought to see in John's Paraclete a human being like Jesus, possessing the faculties of hearing and speech formally implied in John's Greek text. Jesus therefore predicts that God will later send a human being to Earth to take up the role defined by John, i.e. to be a prophet who hears God's word and repeats his message to man. This is the logical interpretation of John's texts arrived at if one attributes to the words their proper meaning.

"The presence of the term 'Holy Spirit' in today's text could easily have come from a later addition made quite deliberately. It may have been intended to change the original meaning which predicted the advent of a prophet subsequent to Jesus and was therefore in contradiction with the teachings of the Christian churches at the time of their formation; these teachings maintained that Jesus was the last of the prophets."[60]

The *Grande Encyclopedie Francaise* has the following to say in its entry on Muhammad, upon whom be blessings and peace: "Muhammad, the founder of the religion of Islam, the Messenger of God and the Seal of the Prophets. The word Muhammad means the one who is praised; it is derived from the root *hamd*, meaning laudation and veneration. By a remarkable coincidence, there is another name, derived from the same root as Muhammad and synonymous with it, Ahmad, which was very probably used by the Christians of Arabia as the equivalent of Paraclete. Ahmad, meaning much praised and revered, is the translation of the word *perikletos* which has been mistakenly rendered as *parakletos*. For this reason, Muslim religious writers have repeatedly remarked that this name refers to the future appearance of the Prophet of Islam. The Quran refers to this matter in a remarkable verse in *Surah Saff*."[61]

The verse referred to by the encyclopedia runs as follows: " *When Jesus son of Mary said to the Children of Israel, 'I am God's Messenger sent unto you. I confirm the veracity of the Torah which is here in front of me and give you glad tidings that a Prophet will come after me whose name is Ahmad.' But when the Prophet came to the people with proofs and miracles, they said, 'This is clear magic.' "(61:6)*

In another verse the Quran says the following: *"Those Jews and Christians will enjoy God's mercy who follow the unlettered Prophet whose description they read in the Torah and the Gospels. He is a Prophet who summons them unto good and restrains them from evil, who makes the pure licit for them and the impure illicit, and releases them from the shackles of heavy and arduous obligations. So those who believe in him, revere him and aid him, and follow his clear and luminous guidance, are in truth on the path of salvation."(6:156)*

Lesson Twenty
The Sealing of Prophethood

The sealing of prophethood has always been regarded as one of the fundamental components of belief in Islam; it negates the possibility of the emergence of any Messenger after the Prophet of Islam.

In any discussion of Islam, we cannot overlook the role played in it by the sealing of prophethood with the Prophet Muhammad. What Muslim is there who does not immediately think of the Prophet's aspect as seal whenever he call him to mind, or who has any doubt that the Quran is the final revealed message of God?

No religion is known to us that like Islam proclaims the sealing of revelation, nor any heavenly personality who has claimed eternal validity for his message.

More than fourteen centuries have passed since the rise of Islam, and throughout this period the Prophet of Islam has always been regarded as the Seal of the Prophets. He perfected existing laws, and with the rich content of his own logical and thorough program of action, he demonstrated the ultimate value inherent in all the prophetic missions.

By contrast with other schools of religious thought, the validity of which was restricted to a certain time or place, Islam represents a comprehensive summation of all prophetic messages, and it recognizes no boundaries, whether spatial or temporal.

The Quran itself also depicts the brilliant visage of Muhammad, upon whom be peace and blessings, as the one by means of whom the gate of prophethood has been closed.

How can we solve the apparent contradiction between the need for Prophets as the condition for the vitality of human existence, on the one hand, and the permanent sealing of prophethood, on the other? How can we reconcile the principle of the immutability of the ordinances of Islam with the principle of social development and the everlasting search for new concepts and norms?

Industrial and technological developments have turned the human being into a creature always desiring novelty, and wishing to connect every aspect of his life to new principles and institutions. How can such a human being organize his social life and development on the basis of a religion that originated more than fourteen centuries ago and summons the human being to recognize a series of fixed and unchanging values? Having expounded the doctrine of the sealing of prophethood, Islam itself provides the answers to these questions.

One of the reasons for the sending of new Prophets was the corruptions and distortions that had crept into the teachings and books of their predecessors, with the result that they lost their efficacy in the guidance of the human being.

But once the human being reaches a stage in his growth where he can preserve the norms and teachings of religion from corruption or change and propagate them in their authentic form, the most fundamental reason for the sending of new Prophets disappears.

The age in which the Prophet of Islam made his appearance thus differs completely from the ages in which earlier Prophets had emerged: the human being had reached a level of intellectual maturity which permitted the sealing of prophethood.

The attainment of maturity by society, the rise of science and learning, and the human being's acquisition of the ability to preserve and propagate heavenly religion—all this meant that an essential precondition for the sealing of prophethood had been met. It was now possible for the duty of propagating religion and guiding people to be entrusted to scholars and learned persons. From now on, it was up to the human being to preserve his historical heritage and spiritual achievements and to protect the final revelation from corruption by seeking aid in the Quran itself and drawing on his cultural and social maturity. Instead of the responsibility being placed on a single individual, the message was now entrusted to a collectivity. As the Quran says: *"There should be a group among you who summon to virtue and enjoin good upon them and restrain them from evil."*(3:104)

In his social development, the human being reaches a stage

where he no longer stands in need of repeated surgical intervention and is instead ready for a form of permanent prophethood where human beings shape their own destiny on the basis of clear vision, correct choice and reflection on the contents of revelation.

Under such conditions, a social and intellectual order is needed that will free the thoughts and acts of human beings from the wearying and stultifying burden of attachment and give shape and direction to their constant exertions in the realm of both thought and action. The eternal miracle that is the Noble Quran sets forth the main principles of such a system by following which human being is able to advance.

Among all the heavenly books the Quran is the only one to have withstood the ravages of time so that we have in our possession a complete and uncorrupted text clearly reflecting its abundantly creative teachings. The Quran itself proclaims: *"We it is Who have sent down this Quran and We it is Who will protect it."*(15:9) This verse indicates that the most important reason for the sending of new Prophets no longer obtains.

In addition, we should be aware that belief in all the Prophets signifies belief in a continuous historical process, one which began with history itself and the origins of human society has expressed itself in a struggle between truth and falsehood and will continue until the final triumph of the former over the latter. In each age, the Prophets have advanced the awareness and maturity of human beings in accordance with the circumstances and capacities of society.

Differences with respect to certain laws and ordinances do not touch on the fundamental principles and nature of religion because this apparent lack of harmony relates to subsidiary matters, not fundamental concern connected with the very nature of religion.

To correct deviations in thought and belief is possible, in fact, only if a variety of programs of action, each congruent with a set of objective realities, are adopted. If an apparent lack of harmony can be observed in the methods followed by the Prophets in the course of their continuous efforts, this has no connection with their fundamental aim. There is no contradiction among their missions with respect to the principal goal—changing and forming anew the thoughts of human beings who had lost touch with reality and were living in darkness, both culturally and socially.

The Glorious Quran says: *"After earlier Prophets, We sent Jesus, son of Mary; he confirmed the Torah brought by Moses."*(5:46)

The Quran Confirms the Mission of Previous Prophets

Not only does the Quran not negate and invalidate previous revelations, it positively confirms the messengerhood of all previous Prophets and true guides, and praises those great men for their efforts and exertions.

In the Quran, the names of those revered by Jews and Christians as their leaders have been mentioned repeatedly and with respect. Does this praise and veneration of those figures not indicate the veracity, truthfulness and trustworthiness of the message of the Quran, as based on revelation? After all, the followers of Judaism and Christianity were intensely hostile to the new religion of Islam, and the fact that the Quran praises the figures sacred to those two religions proves how far removed the Quran is from all petty rivalry and how alien to it are all kinds of power-seeking.

The Quran proclaims: *"We have sent this book down to you in truth, confirming, verifying and protecting the previous heavenly books."*(5:48)

Since religion is rooted in the essential disposition of the human being, as one of his fundamental impulses that find expression in his view of the world and his deeds, it is basically one and unvarying. The Noble Quran says: *"Turn directly towards religion, for God has created the human being's fundamental disposition in accordance with it."* (30:29)

So although the human being is subject to the norms that prevail in the phenomenal world and gains meaning by entering into relationship with those phenomena and the law of growth toward perfection that governs them, his path to happiness is single and unique. It is religion alone that can show him the specific path to a specific goal. Montesquieu says: "It is in the very nature of human laws that they obey events and occurrences. That is to say, events influence them. By contrast, heavenly laws do not change on the basis of events or the changing will of the human being. Human laws always aim at attaining the best of solutions; heavenly laws actually discover the best of solutions. Virtue and goodness have, no doubt, many different aspects and varieties, but the best of all solutions is necessarily unique and also, therefore, immutable. The human being can change human laws because it is possible that a given law be beneficial in one age but not in another. Religious systems always offer the best laws and because they cannot be improved upon, they are unchangeable."[62]

If we turn our backs on Divine Laws and have recourse to man-made regulations, we have, in fact, abandoned the broad and open plain of the universal law of religion for the narrow and uneven alley that is the limited mind of the human being.

The fundamental difference between the mission of the Prophet of Islam and that of the other Prophets lies in the fact that their revelation served as the basis for a temporary program of action. Once Islam made its appearance and earlier religious systems had begun to weaken and crumble, it was no longer possible to adhere to those religions and systems of belief.

The value-system of Islam, by contrast, completes the whole structure of prophethood: its logical coherence and unshakeable firmness embrace all the extensive dimensions of prophethood, and it includes within itself all that the preceding Prophets put forward to satisfy the human being's needs for social regulation, as well as all other moral and material needs.

The role that the Prophets played in correcting the errors and deviations of society and establishing a correct mode of thought and action is now to be assumed by the religious leaders who draw on the inexhaustible resources of Islam. The Quran, the value-system of which nurtures the whole of Islam and endows it with validity, also determines the direction in which the Muslims are to advance and serves as the source of comprehensive laws which leave nothing beyond their all-embracing purview. In addition, the Quran contains the essence and fundamental meaning of the teachings proclaimed by all the bearers of God's word.

Once the human being reaches a stage in his development where he is able to comprehend universal truths and Divine teachings and laws, the scholars and the learned emerge as successors to the Prophets, with the function of firmly implanting the authentic criteria of religion in the minds of people.

In pursuit of the exalted ideals of their religion, they take on the tasks of investigation and research and struggling against distortion of religion; they propagate the teachings of God in their true form.

In many verses of the Quran, human beings are invited to study natural phenomena with care, in order to perceive by way of deduction the spirit that rules over the scheme of creation.

The constant attention paid by the Quran to reason and experience and their utility and the significance it accords to nature and history as sources for the attainment of knowledge, are connected them with the sealing of prophethood by the Quran and the Prophet of Islam. They indicate the prevalence of a new worldview in the history of mankind.

Abstract goals must inevitably be transformed into objective realities if they are to have validity. We see, indeed, that for almost fifteen centuries the human being has proven his ability to assume these heavy but fruitful responsibilities by preserving his religious and scientific heritage and exhibiting both profundity and realism in analyzing and interpreting it.

This is in itself an indication of the human being's attainment of independence and his readiness to preserve the Divine verses with utmost care and his ability to assume the duty of propagating, interpreting, teaching and disseminating religion.

Once the final Divine Command had reached the human being, there was no possibility for the coming of a new Messenger. The sealing of revelation may be compared to the case of a certain piece of land where all necessary archaeological excavations have been carried out with the utmost care to unearth ancient artifacts. There is nothing left hidden in the earth to justify new research and digging.

Once prophethood has passed through different stages to reach its final degree of perfection and exaltedness, and from the point of view of revelation all the dark and obscure matters that lie within the range of human thought and comprehension have been clarified, there is no road left to be travelled, no explanation to be made. Prophethood has fulfilled its role and reached its final destination. Nonetheless, its life continues by means of the inexhaustibility of revelation, which provides a single social, cultural and value system beyond the confines of time.

The Prophet of Islam proclaims, in a clear and pleasing fashion: "Prophethood is like a house, the building of which has now been completed. There is room for only one more brick, and I am putting that brick in its place."[63]

Although the mission of the Prophets to proclaim the Divine message and aid humanity came to an end with the blossoming and maturity of human thought, the spiritual relationship between the world of the human being and the world of the unseen has never been severed. The human being's path to exalted station necessarily continues to pass through the purification of the spirit and the cultivation of sincere devotion to God.

The human being has numerous creative dimensions, and it is only through sustained spiritual effort that he will be able to actualize his potential capacities. He will then enter into communication with the world of the unseen and see and know what those who are absorbed in the outer appearances of the material world cannot see and know. It is again such spiritual effort that gives the human being a truly human aspect, enables him to appear as God's viceregent on earth, and grants him access to values that give his life meaning and content.

Numerous, therefore, are those persons who have a high degree of religiosity and abundant spirituality without attaining the lofty degree of prophethood and the religious leadership of mankind.

The doors of illumination and inspiration are open to all those who wish to purify their inner beings of the pollution and darkness of sin and who turn their hearts toward the life-giving breeze of Divine knowledge.

Spiritual grace is never cut off from the human being, nor does it suffer any decrease. The degree to which the human being may benefit from it, in a direct and profound way, depends only on his spiritual capacity and abilities. These determine the extent to which he may draw on the unceasing and limitless favor and grace of God.

Lesson Twenty-one
An Answer to the Materialists

The materialists say to us: "Since change and development are regarded as the most fundamental and pervasive law of nature, nothing in the world enjoying stability, the principles of change cannot be reconciled with the claim of Islam to eternal validity."

The first part of this statement is correct and entirely defensible. However, it does not represent the entire truth of the matter. It is true that everything in the world is subject to change, but that which is changing in nature and destined to disappear is matter and the phenomena arising from it, not the laws and systems prevailing in nature. Both the natural order and the social order (insofar as it corresponds to natural norms) are exempt from change; universality and atemporality are among the defining characteristics of laws. It is these properties that give laws the ability to retain their validity.

Stars and planets come into being, rotate, disseminate light and energy, and finally are extinguished. However, the law of gravity that governs them remains in force.

The human being enters the world, in accordance with a Divine custom and norm and the general movement of all things toward perfection, and after passing through his allotted lifespan, weakens and dies. Death is the inevitable end of every human being, but the laws that govern the human being and the world that surrounds outlive him.

Numerous sources of heat, at different temperatures, appear in the world and then become cold, but the law of heat is not extinguished.

If natural man is the object envisaged when drawing up laws and his fundamental structure and disposition are kept in mind by the lawgiver, temporal changes can never induce the slightest change in this kind of law, because the essence and fundamental substance of the human being is unchanging.

The founder of Islam has closed his eyes on the world, but the Divine Law he brought remains eternally valid, because it draws on the very nature of the human being. This is the secret of the stability and permanence of the laws of Islam.

Islam is not a political and social phenomenon. It represents a series of principles, together with their derivatives, that are illumined by the primal light of all existence. It is a law and a worldview which in the very nature of things cannot change its character.

Islam is not a religion for a certain season or place or race; it belongs neither to the Arabs nor to the non-Arabs. The words of the Quran are addressed to the whole of humanity: *"O mankind, We have created you out of a man and a woman and made of you different lineages so that you might recognize each other. The greatest of human beings in God's sight is the most pious."*(49:12) *"Oh sons of Adam! Let not Satan deceive you, as he drove your father and mother from Paradise and stripped from them the garment of dignity."*(7:25)

Holding fast to immutable laws despite the advances made in science and civilization and the changes that appear in certain human needs does not involve any problem. For throughout the process of his development, the human being continues to be subject to needs that arise from the very nature of his life and the depths of his spirit or are connected with his bodily structure. Their trace is to be seen everywhere in history and they are marked by continuity and permanence. As long as the human being continues to live on this planet, change will never affect the essence of the human being or those elements in him which form the nucleus of his desires.

There is another set of needs relations to the human being's exploitation of nature and the resources he needs for his welfare, and others again touching on the blossoming of his creative capacities. Here, the occurrence of a new set of circumstances may indeed change the conditions of life: developments in technology, for example, may confront society with new wishes and desires. It is in areas such as this that change and transformation occur, not in the sphere outlined above.

This means that the human being should not sacrifice all the authentic and valuable criteria he has inherited to changing spatial and temporal circumstance, and that he should not turn his back on what is truly creative in the name of a facile innovativeness.

Change and innovation in needed tools and instruments, made necessary by the development of civilization, do indeed involve a series of secondary laws and regulations. It is up to those who are specialized in Islamic concerns to determine those laws, based on the specific conditions of the time, to deduce them from the fixed and general principles of the law, and to implement them.

Laws of temporary validity can, then, be drawn up for matters that are subject to change, but not for those that are immutable. The legislative system of Islam maintains a clear distinction between the two categories.

For example, Islam has assigned to the just and competent Islamic government broad powers in deciding on matters relating to the preservation of internal security, commercial relations, political relations with foreign countries, questions of defense and mobilization, public health and so on—all of these being matters which cannot be beneficially regulated outside of the framework set by the realities of the day.

These are all changeable matters, relating to the superstructure of society; their nature may change at any time. Islam, therefore, with the vitality and dynamism that characterize it, has not laid down laws for matters subject to change, providing instead general and comprehensive criteria to which to refer.

Such an approach is capable of bringing about a profound transformation in the life of society, enabling it to exploit more fully the resources of nature and to raise the general level of awareness. But the laws of Islam relating to the sphere that derives from principles and characteristics essential to the human being are tied up with his very nature, are fixed and not exposed to the tempest of spatio-temporal change.

For example, the love and affection of a father and mother for their child represents one continuous and permanent manifestation of the essential disposition of the human being, and rights such as those of inheritance which derive from this relationship of love are necessarily eternal. Likewise, the need of the human being to establish a family is a general and universal one, and throughout history his life has always taken on a collective form.

So from the very first day that the saplings of thought and

reflecting grew from the human spirit, throughout all the vicissitudes of history and the rise and fall of civilizations, indications are to be found that the human being was always social by nature, in all the different stages of his development, and always had the need to establish a family.

The relevant criteria and ordinances must therefore be of permanent validity, for the human being's tendencies today are intermingled with the past in the depths of his essence. The existential fabric of the human being, his distinctive inward nature, will never undergo a substantial or fundamental change; nothing will prevent it from continuing on its appointed and unchanging path.

For matters such as family relationships and social relationships in general, and the rights of individuals, Islam has therefore established fixed and unchanging laws. If these laws be based on justice and are rooted in the depths of human nature, why should they be changed or modified? In what direction, away from justice and conformity to human nature, should they be made to develop?

In addition, fundamental concepts such as conscientiousness, trustworthiness, or negative attributes such as oppressiveness, treacherousness and mendacity, are also fixed and constant, both in their individual and their collective manifestation. Permanence and constancy must then be extended also to the laws relating to them, although the method of implementing those laws may be subject to change.

Therefore those laws have value and validity that have been drawn up with attention to the true nature of the human being and his ineluctable destiny, that relate him to the universal movement of all beings as well as to the specific aim for which he was created. Such laws are capable, in every age, of helping people live constructively, to administer their affairs properly and to attain true guidance.

If Islam has not promulgated laws of eternal validity for the human being's efforts to satisfy his needs, it is because failure to take into consideration the changing nature of such concerns when formulating the law would be a weakness, just as the failure to take into consideration the human being's unchanging inner disposition in other matters is also a weakness.

We know as well that the human being is himself an abundant

source of social and environmental factors. He may endow himself with great value and loftiness, but at the same time he is not immune to deviation and error and their harmful consequences. Sometimes he may advance in the direction of his true interests, while at other times he rebels, to the detriment of his interests.

It is necessary for him to believe that not every newly appearing phenomenon is an acceptable manifestation of civilization, once measured against his system of values; such an assumption would be impossible to support logically.

The human being attains value only when he combines the acceptance of progress with a creative role in modifying or controlling its products and continues to struggle against all that leads ultimately to the destruction of his true happiness.

Not only is Islam not opposed to whatever may lead a person to a better and happier life, it promises a reward to all who strive to bring that about, for it believes that the world should advance toward the fullest possible development of the human mind. It is precisely this belief that serves as an important factor in bringing about movements for the constructive development of the human being.

A matter that has received particular attention in Islam is the spirit and meaning of life and the paths that lead to the attainment of that ideal. Islam has therefore left people free in choosing the outward shape and form of their lives, which enables them to select their own path forward in coping with the demands of the age in which they live and the deficiencies and contradictions they inevitably encounter. Thus at each new stage they reach a higher and broader level than before.

Since Islam aims at the perfecting of human beings and at the same time bases itself on realities, it regards it as indispensable that the law be linked with reason, and assigns reason such value that it counts it as a source of legal ordinances. On the basis of specific and precise criteria, it assigns to reason the solution of certain problems.

Another matter which gives permanency to the teachings of Islam and vitality and dynamism to its ordinances consists of the extensive powers that have been accorded to the just Islamic government. so that people will know at all times what is required of them, the government is permitted to draw up appropriate laws that are consonant with the needs of the time, whenever new situations require this. In doing this, the government must refer to the established general principles of the law.

The assignation of such powers to the Islamic government is in order to permit experts in Islamic affairs to adopt a suitable attitude to newly occurring circumstances. Employing their intellects free of any restraint and engaging in independent judgement (*ijtihad*) they seek to solve the needs of society as determined by the changing nature of modern life and the unceasing advances of technology in a manner conformable to the unchanging principles of the *shariah*. For change forces the life of society into new channels and gives it a whole new aspect. This principle permits us to solve even the gravest and most complex of problems.

Not only do the true interests of Islamic society and its protection against corruption form the principal consideration in drawing up laws and issuing ordinances, but the greater the degree to which a law serves that purpose, the more it is preferred. Basing itself on this principle, Islam has permitted the scholars and jurists, whenever they encounter a situation in which two interests contradict each other, to sacrifice the lesser interest in favor of the greater, thus solving their dilemma.

Similarly, whenever circumstances turn a religious command into an imposition beyond the human being's power, a person is relieved of the responsibility for carrying it out.

All these are factors which give flexibility and vitality to Islam, and enable it to retain unlimited validity and the ability to advance together with the progress of human life.

It is a mistake to imagine that determining historical factors necessarily place a limit on the validity of a given law or system. The extent to which those determining historical factors actually exercise an effect must be assessed to see whether a given law actually enjoys permanence or not, for the effect of a particular historical factor depends on the type of that force: if the force enjoys permanence, so will its effect; and if it does not, neither will its effect.

One factor in history is the historical factor; belief in religion has been a constant norm of history. Attachment to the source and origin of existence is something that wells up from the human being's inner being, and it plays a role in differing ways in all the successive stages of his life. The natural norms of history have themselves determined that religion should always retain a permanent and autonomous identity in human life.

The point of view that this suggests gives us the possibility of looking at things in a certain way, and to make choices accordingly. It would be a sign of extreme fanaticism to imagine that regarding all facts from a single point of view furnishes an adequate criterion for judging and assessing things—to assume, for example, that economics alone is the sole basic factor throughout history.

Some people are of the opinion that the economic factor plays a uniquely determining role, that impervious to people's will it can destroy all value systems and change all situations as it pleases. But we must ask what role people play in the unfolding of this determining role. Does the human being's free will and choice—that which distinguishes him from all material phenomena—have anything to do with this ineluctable process?

The Prophets never surrendered to the bitter realities that confronted them. Realism in assessing the environment in which they operated did not prevent them from setting certain goals and acting to achieve them; they were never tempted to justify everything by invoking historical determinism.

Golzerman, a famous scholars says: "In just the same way that it would be wrong to deny absolutely all necessity in history, it would also be wrong to accept that everything in history is determined."[64]

No realistic person will base his judgment on the principle that a self-sacrificing person who is overflowing with love, who changes the values and criteria of the human being, who looks pityingly on all forms of indolence, arrogance, greed and animal pleasure, who is constantly advancing towards creativity, perfection, nobility, wisdom and justice—that such a person is in fact a mono-dimensional being, imprisoned in the confines of his personality and a prisoner to objects. It is such an assumption that underlies the assertion that economics alone is the determining factor in religion, science, philosophy, ethics, and all other aspects of life.

To judge matters in this way is far from objective. Those who dogmatically assume such positions and insist on their own point of view as furnishing a comprehensive and neutral interpretation of the whole of history have abandoned all fairness and justice.

Notes

1. *Mas'ala-yi Vahy*, p. 31.
2. Allama Majlisi, *Bihar al-Anwar*, Vol. XI, p. 60.
3. Will Durant, *The Story of Civilization*.
4. Alexis Carrel, *Insan, Maujud-i-Nashinakhta*, pp. 2, 3, 7, 149.
5. *Qaradad-i Ijtima'i (The Social Contract)*, p. 81.
6. Carrel, *op. cit.*, p. 30.
7. *Bihar al-Anwar*, Vol. XI, p. 70.
8. *Nahj al-Balagha*, ed. Muhammad Abduh, pp. 57-60.
9. Allama Muhammad Iqbal, *The Reconstruction of Religious Thought in Islam*, ed. M. Saeed Sheikh, Lahore, 1986, p. 99.
10. *Jahan va Einstein*, p. 130.
11. Gospel of St. Matthew, 5:17.
12. *Amali as-Saduq*, p. 376.
13. *Bihar al-Anwar*, Vol. LXX, p. 211.
14. *Sirat ibn Hisham*, Vol. I, p. 162.
15. *Ibid.*, p. 179.
16. *Tarikh-i Tabari*, Vol. I, pp. 33-34.
17. *Ibid.*, Vol. II, p. 1138.
18. *Sirat ibn Hisham*, Vol. I.
19. *Mas'udi, Muruj adh-Dhahab*, Vol. I, p. 400.
20. *Tarikh-i Tabari*, Vol. II, p. 1172; ibn Athir, *al-Kamil*, Vol. II, p. 40; ibn Hanbal, *Musnad*, p. 111.
21. Halabi, *Sira*, p. 334.
22. *Sirat ibn Hisham*, Vol. I, p. 338.
23. *Ibid.*, p. 278.
24. al-Ya'qubi, *Tarikh*, Vol. II, p. 17.
25. *Majma' al-Bayan*, Vol. I, p. 387.
26. *Sirat ibn Hisham*, Vol. I, p. 480.
27. *Nahj al-Balagha*, ed. Fayz, p. 83.
28. Jawaharlal Nehru, *Glimpses of World History*, New York,

1948, pp. 142, 144.

29. Maurice Bucaille, *The Bible, the Quran and Science*, Indianapolis, 1976, pp. 148-149. Italics are author's.

30. *Sirat ibn Hisham*, Vol. I, p. 386.

31. Muhammad, *Payghambari ki az nau bayad shinakht*, p. 45.

32. Iqbal, *op. cit.*, pp. 101-102.

33. Bucaille, *op. cit.*, pp. 115-116, 119, 121-122, 125.

34. *Sarguzasht-i Zamin*, p. 43.

35. *Nujum-i bi-tiliskup*, p., 83.

36. Bucaile, *op. cit.*, pp. 143-144, 147, 150.

37. *Jahan va Einstein*, p. 112.

38. *Az kahkashan ta insan*, p. 47.

39. *Danishmandan-i Buzurg-i Jahan-i Ilm*, p. 49.

40. *Tafsir-i Burhan*, Vol. II, p. 278.

41. Bucaille, *op. cit.*

42. *Majalla-yi Danishmand*, Vol. IX, no. 4.

43. *Tasvir-i Jahan dar Fizik-i Jadid*, p. 95.

44. Bucaille, *op. cit.*, p. 120.

45. *Tarikh-i Ulum va Adabiyat dar Iran*, pp. 3-4.

46. *Majma al-Bayan*, Vol. VIII, p. 295.

47. *al-Quran wa 'l-Ulum al-Islamiyya*, p. 4.

48. *Usul al-Kafi*, p. 591.

49. *Muhammad va Quran.*

50. *Isbat-i Vujud-i Khuda*, p. 58.

51. *Ibid.*, p. 230.

52. Gospel of St. John, 14:30.

53. *Ibid.*, 15:26.

54. *Ibid.*, 16:7-14.

55. *Ibid.*, 14:26.

56. In fact, for John it was during the Last Supper itself that Jesus delivered the long speech that mentions the Paraclete.

57. Nestle and Aland. Pub. United Bibles Societies, London, 1971.

58. This manuscript was written in the Fourth or Fifth century A.D. It was discovered in 1812 on Mount Sinai by Agnes S. Lewis and is so named because the first text had been covered by a later one which, when obliterated, revealed the original.

59. Many translations and commentaries of the Gospel, especially older ones, use the word 'Consoler' to translate this,

but it is totally inaccurate.
60. Bucaille, *op. cit.*, pp. 102-106.
61. Vol. XXIII, p. 4174.
62. *L'esprit des lois* (Persian translation), p. 725.
63. *Majma al-Bayan* on Ahzab, 40.
64. *Ilm-i Tahavvul-i Jami'a.*

General Index